MODERN MUSIC NOTATION

A
Reference and Textbook

by

Laszlo Boehm

SCHIRMER BOOKS
A Division of Macmillan Publishing Co., Inc.
NEW YORK

COLLIER MACMILLAN PUBLISHERS
LONDON

Copyright © 1961 by Schirmer Books
A Division of Macmillan Publishing Co., Inc.

All rights reserved. No part of this book may be reproduced or transmitted in any form or by any means, electronic or mechanical, including photocopying, recording, or by any information storage and retrieval system, without permission in writing from the Publisher.

SCHIRMER BOOKS
A Division of Macmillan Publishing Co., Inc.
866 Third Avenue, New York, N.Y. 10022

Collier Macmillan Canada, Ltd.

Printed in the United States of America

printing number
1 2 3 4 5 6 7 8 9 10

Preface

The notation of music, like any other living means of communication, is constantly changing. New symbols are introduced and find general acceptance, old ones outlive their usefulness. The efforts of generations of music editors and engravers have borne fruit in procedures that present the composer's thought as clearly and cleanly and unequivocally as our admittedly still imperfect system permits.

These symbols and procedures, as they are employed today in the best-edited publications, are described in the following pages. Everyone who writes music down has had occasion to wonder whether a beam should be drawn horizontal or slanted; if slanted, up or down. Does this stem go up or down? Does that chord-note belong to the right of the stem or to the left? Must every eighth note in a vocal part have its own flag? What is the best way to abbreviate "harpsichord"? What is the sign for double tonguing?

Such are only a few of the questions answered in the following pages. The book deals with all the general practical problems of music notation as well as with the special symbols associated with particular instruments. It also gives many tables showing the range of each instrument and type of voice, the various keys and their signatures in the various clefs, the terminology (in six languages) of note values and rests, and other matters, as well as a transposing table of modal scales. In addition to a general index, there is a special index of musical signs — the first one, so far as is known, of its kind.

This manual of modern notation should be of enormous assistance to anyone who wants to read or write music.

Contents

PREFACE iii

   I. SIGNS GENERALLY USED IN MUSIC 1
      The dot — The wedge-shaped stroke — The short horizontal line — The marcato — The sforzato — The tie or slur — The crescendo and decrescendo — The repetition marks — Prima volta and Seconda volta — The octave-mark — Ornaments — The modern tenor clef.

  II. SIGNS USED IN NOTATION OF STRING MUSIC 8
      Simple bowing — Spiccato — Martellato or secco — Détaché — Half spiccato or half tenuto — Staccato — Saltato — Arpeggio — Ricochet — Louré — Legato — Pizzicato — Tremolo effects — Col legno — Sul ponticello — Sul tasto — Numbering of strings — Con sordino and senza sordino.

 III. SIGNS USED IN NOTATION OF WIND MUSIC 14
      Single, double, triple tonguing — Flutter tonguing — Messa di voce — Stopped tones on the horn — Open playing — Con sord. and senza sord. in horns, trumpets, and trombone parts.

 IV. SIGNS USED IN NOTATION FOR PERCUSSION INSTRUMENTS 16
      Timpani — Glockenspiel — Xylophone — Celesta — Vibraphone — Triangle — Snare and Tenor drums — Bass drum — Cymbals — Tambourine — Gong.

  V. SIGNS COMMONLY USED IN HARP, PIANO, AND ORGAN MUSIC 19
      Arpeggio — Let vibrate — Glissando — Harmonics on the harp — Piano pedaling — Una corda and tre corde — Toe and heel.

 VI. THE RANGE OF MUSICAL INSTRUMENTS AND THE HUMAN VOICES
      A. Woodwinds 23
      B. Brass 26
      C. Strings 27
      D. Miscellaneous instruments 28
      E. Percussion of definite pitch 29
      F. Percussion of indefinite pitch 30
      G. Mixed choruses 31

VII. THE TECHNIQUE OF CORRECT MODERN MUSICAL NOTATION 33

VIII. TABLES
    1. Terminology of note values and rests 60
    2. The names and symbols for octaves 62
    3. The division of note values 63
    4. A general view of the keys and key signatures 64
    5. The location of key signatures on the staff in alto, tenor, and bass clefs 66
    6. Transposing table of Modal Scales 67

INDEX OF SIGNS 68

GENERAL INDEX 69

I
Signs Generally Used in Music

A **dot** over or under a note indicates the ordinary **staccato** (abbr.: stacc.). The notes marked with this *staccato-mark* are to be played short, separated, disconnected; they are not to be sustained for their full time value. The mood of the staccato is in sharp contrast to tenuto and legato (see page 2).

A dot set after the note-head prolongs its time value by half:

Two dots prolong the time value by three quarters:

Three dots set after the note-head further prolong its time value by half of the second dot. The use of three dots is quite rare and almost unnecessary:

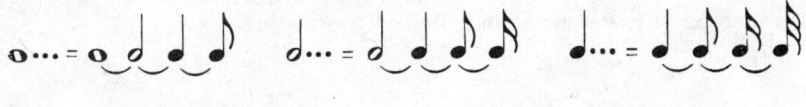

A wedge-shaped stroke over a note generally indicates **staccatissimo**, a very short, sharp staccato employed mostly in loud music.

This sign in string music indicates martellato or secco (see page 8).

A short horizontal line above or below the note generally indicates **tenuto** (abbr.: ten.). The notes so marked are to be sustained for their full time value.

This sign over or under a note, called **marcato**, indicates a strongly accented forte sound, diminishing instantly to piano. When the mark occurs in soft music, it indicates only a slight accent. The letters *fp*, meaning forte-piano, are sometimes substituted for this sign.

The mark for **sforzato** (abbr.: *sfz* or *fz*) or **rinforzando** (abbr.: *rinf.* or *rfz*) means forcing or reinforcing as a special emphasis. The mark indicates a sudden and very strong accent on a *single note* or *chord*. There is practically no difference between sforzato and rinforzando.

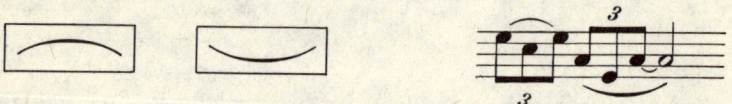

The curved line is called a **tie** or a **slur**, according to its function. If it connects two *neighboring* notes on the *same* pitch, the two notes are to be sounded as one, equal to their united time value:

Here the curved line is a tie, because it serves to tie the two notes together.

If the curved line is drawn over (or under) notes of *different* pitch, the notes so marked are to be performed *legato*, i.e. in a smooth and connected manner, with no break between them. In this case the name of the curved line is legato-mark or legato-slur.

But the curved line indicates also that a group or series of notes are to be executed on one syllable in vocal music, in one breath in wind parts (and in vocal music also); it indicates the number of notes to be taken on a single stroke of the bow on stringed instruments, or even marks a musical phrase. Frequently the curved line is used in its several meanings at the same time. In such cases they should be placed carefully because their sequence is important. See the example below, a few bars taken from a vocal composition. This illustrates all the rules for the use of ties and slurs, rules that are applicable in instrumental writing also.

1 indicates *tied notes;* 2 shows the length of one syllable, which consequently has to be sung in *one breath;* 3 marks the *musical phrase.* The order of numbers shows the sequence of drawing the slurs also.

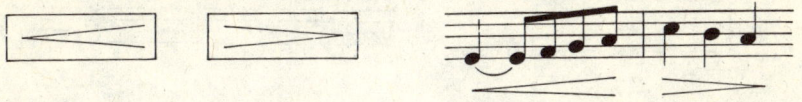

The first mark above indicates **crescendo** (abbr.: cresc.), *increasing in loudness,* i.e. p to f (piano to forte), mf to ff (mezzoforte to fortissimo), etc. The second mark above indicates the reverse of the first: **decrescendo** (abbr.: decresc.), i.e. diminishing in loudness from f to p, mf to pp, etc. Both signs are used for short crescendo or decrescendo effects only, underneath the notes. If the dynamic effect desired includes two or more bars, modern notation uses the abbreviations cresc. or decresc. If the effect is especially long the best method is to write out the whole instruction beneath the notes in separated syllables like this:

cre................scen................do

de................cre................scen................do

When this method is used, the dynamic level towards which the effect moves must always be indicated.

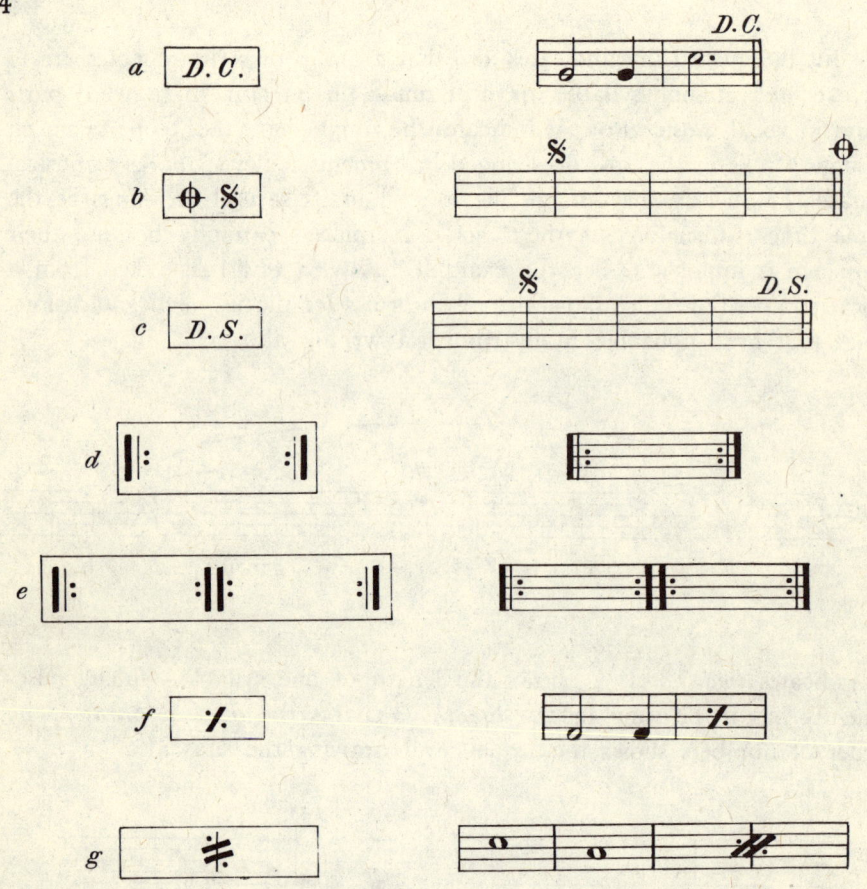

These are the common **repetition marks** of a section or of a bar. Under a) is the **Da Capo** ("from the head"; abbreviated: D.C.). When the performer reaches this mark, he must turn back to the *beginning* of the piece and repeat the whole section.

The two signs at b) indicate the repetition of the section between the marks ⊕ and 𝄋 . When the performer reaches the mark ⊕ , he must go back to the place marked 𝄋 and perform the whole section again Sometimes the abbrevation under c) is used for the same purpose. The "D.S." stands for **Dal Segno,** "from the sign." In such cases the performer plays until reaching the D.S., then goes back to the "sign" 𝄋 and plays the section again. The most common repetition mark, under d), is not to be confused with the barline. A repetition mark could be somewhere *within* the bar too. All bars between the two thick lines are to be repeated, performed in exactly the same manner as the first time.

The **double repetition mark** e) divides a section into two parts and calls for the repetition of each part as explained under d).

The mark at f) indicates the **repeat of the preceding bar.** It always stands in the middle of an empty bar.

For the **repetition of two bars** the mark at g) is used. The marks f) and g) are used mostly in orchestral parts. For notation see page 50.

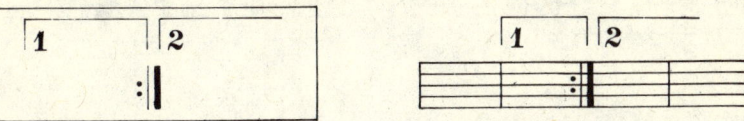

This mark — **prima volta, seconda volta** ("the first time, the second time") — indicates different endings for the first and second performance of a repeated section. The measure or measures under its bracket with the numeral 1 are to be played the first time, before the repeat, whereas on repeating, those marked 2 are to be performed *instead*.

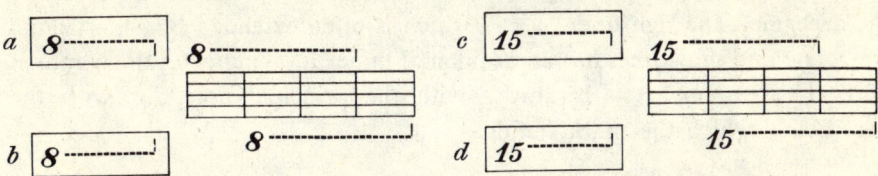

These marks — the numeral 8 (as in a) and b)) or 15 (as in c) and d)) connected with a short or long, sometimes very long, dotted line, above or beneath the staff — indicate that all the notes directly under or over the dotted line have to be performed, according to the given numeral, one or two octaves higher or lower than written. The numeral at the beginning of the dotted line denotes the required interval — one octave or, rarely, two octaves (the interval of two octaves is indicated by 15, *not* 16!). The dotted line at the end of the transposition must be closed down by a short vertical line. After this closing down the notes are to be performed at the written pitch, as is shown below:

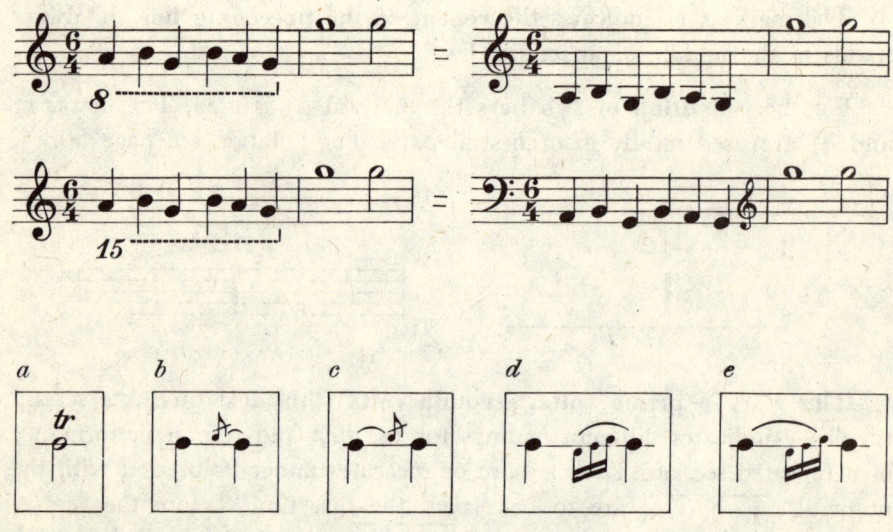

Modern notation uses only the types of embellishments shown above and the arpeggio. The sign under a) — which is often extended by a horizontal wavy line and sometimes has an accidental under it — indicates the common **trill**. This ornament starts always with the principal note, i.e. with the note above which the mark stands:

The modern trill, a virtuoso effect, usually has a two-tone termination, as in the example. For special notation of the trill see page 46.

The modern **appoggiatura** (see b) and c) above), which is very quick, is indicated by a small eighth note with a single stroke across its stem. To avoid doubt as to whether the appoggiatura should be performed accented on the beat (as at b) below) or unaccented before the beat (as in c) below), modern notation uses a small slur. This slur indicates the note from which the short time value of the grace-note is taken:

Short grace-note figures (d) and e) above) are also connected by a slur with the note from which the time of their performance is taken:

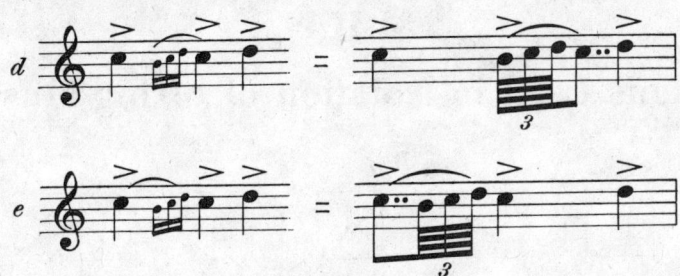

In cases of longer ornamental passages it is best to write out each note in its exact time value.

Caution. — All these rules for ornamentation are only valid in modern notation and are *not* applicable for reading older music.

This **modern tenor clef** is used solely for tenor voice parts. The numeral 8 underneath the common violin clef signifies that the part lies an octave lower than written:

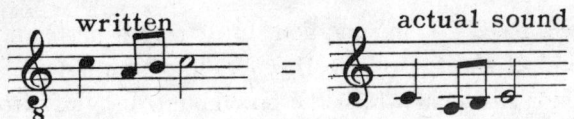

II
Signs Used in Notation of String Music

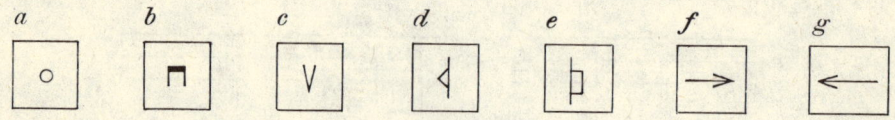

These signs are the most common ones used in string music — that is, music for the violin, the viola, the 'cello, and the double bass. The marks indicate:

a) **Open string** or **harmonics,** the latter mostly with the abbreviation "harm." above it;

b) **Down-bow;**

c) **Up-bow;**

d) With the **tip of the bow;**

e) On the **frog or nut;**

f) With the **upper half of the bow;**

g) With the **lower half of the bow.**

The last four signs are used generally in notation for beginners. The sign indicating an open string — a) — is used in harp and guitar notation also.

A dot (see page 1) in notation for stringed instruments indicates **spiccato,** a kind of short stroke in the middle of the bow in quick tempo. This is a brilliant effect, in which the bow bounces slightly from the string.

On a stringed instrument the wedge (ᵥ see page 1) indicates **martellato** (literally a "hammered" stroke) or **secco,** mostly in loud passages. The effect is obtained by releasing each stroke forcefully and suddenly. The notes so marked are to be played with very short bows at the point or with a hard, vigorous stroke near the frog.

In notation for stringed instruments the tenuto mark (—) indicates a kind of stroke called **détaché** (or also tenuto, see page 2), i.e., "detched." This is the playing of successive notes with a slight articulation of the rapidly alternating down-bow and up-bow, but holding the full time value of the notes, never staccato. The détaché is not good at great speed.

The mark is sometimes combined with the staccato-mark like this

indicating for strings the so-called **half-spiccato** or **half-tenuto**. This is a special stroke, played by separating the notes so marked with a half-bouncing bow, holding almost the full time value of the notes.

a
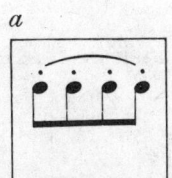
b
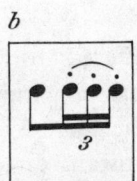
c
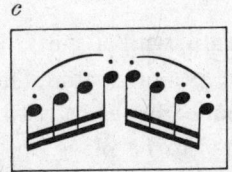
d
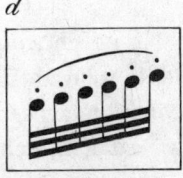

In the notation of stringed instruments the slur is often connected with other marks, mostly the dot and tenuto-mark, indicating several kinds of bowing.

1. The slur with dots beneath it:

a) **Staccato.** This consists of a number of martellato notes taken in the same stroke. A brilliant effect, executed mostly with up-bow.

b) **Saltato,** i.e. two or more notes executed by a single bouncing stroke.

c) **Arpeggio,** almost the same as b) but using several strings.

d) **Ricochet.** This is a down-stroke which is done by throwing the upper third of the bow on the same string, resulting in a bouncing series of rapid notes (usually no more than six) in one stroke.

2. The slur with a tenuto-mark beneath it:

indicates a stroke called **louré.** This is a slurred, legato effect useful in slow tempo to separate slightly each of the notes under the slur. It may be used in down-bow and up-bow.

For **legato** bowing, see page 3.

Pizzicato is done by plucking the strings with the fingers. The duration of the resulting tone is quite short. It has no special mark beside the written abbreviation: pizz. This indication remains valid until the new indication appears: arco (the Italian word for "bow"), which means play with the bow:

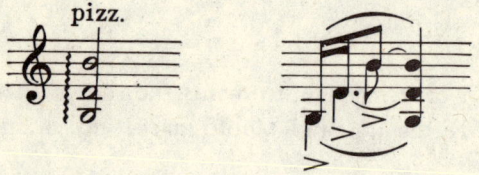

The **chord-pizzicato** with a guitar-like effect consists of at least three tones played in arpeggio-pizzicato. The mark for indicating this is the common arpeggio mark (a vertical wavy line alongside the chord) and, as usual, the chord has to be played in an upward direction:

Sometimes in special **arpeggio-pizzicato** effects it is necessary to mark the *direction* of the arpeggio. There are two ways to do this; with arrows pointing up or down, or with opposite direction of stems:

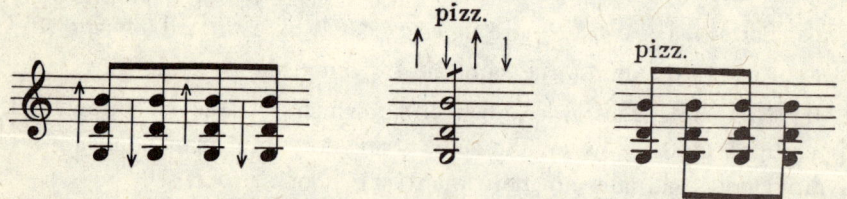

The pizzicato may be connected with the glissando effect too. But the **glissando-pizzicato** may not be longer than the interval of a fifth, because the sound of the pizzicato is very short and, once the string is plucked, dies away very quickly. The note on which the effect begins is always to be written out (this note will be plucked), as is the note on which the effect ends. Between these two notes is the mark of the glissando: the oblique line connecting the two note-heads with the abbreviation "gliss." The starting note is usually marked with a marcato, because this note must be properly accented for best glissando results:

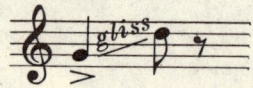

It is possible to perform pizzicato and arco at the same time. In such cases the pizzicato is played with the left hand on the fingerboard, while the right hand plays with the bow. The sign for this effect — **pizzicato with the left hand** — is a small cross above or below the plucked note:

Pizzicato can be used **on harmonics** too. This effect has no special mark; the desired harmonics must be written out with the abbreviation pizz.

If an especially **long vibration of pizzicato** has to be used (in which, after the string is plucked, the vibration is maintained by rapid oscillation of the finger on the string), the vibrating note is marked with a marcato sign and with a short horizontal slur:

Pizzicato on an interval is executed with two plucking fingers. The mark for this effect — besides the abbreviation "pizz." — is a vertical hook connecting the two notes on the left side of the interval:

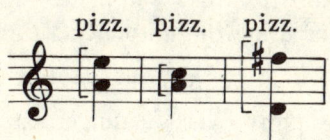

Tremolo effects are produced by the extremely rapid alternation of a very short down-bow and up-bow with the *upper end* of the bow. There are no special signs to mark them, but they are always indicated as a series of fast notes (32nds or 64ths). In the examples below a) indicates **tremolos on single notes,** b) **tremolos on intervals sounded at the same time,** and c) **tremolos on intervals with separated tones,** in which the finger plays an important role too:

The real tremolo is never measured although there are tremolo-like effects notated almost in the same manner as c) above. If the "tremolo" *is* measured, usually an appropriate number shows the quantity of alternations:

To avoid mistakes the abbreviation "trem." usually is added, meaning unmeasured repetition of notes, and "non trem.," meaning limited and prescribed repetitions according to note values as shown above.

For rules of correct notation of tremolos see page 51.

The **col legno** effect ("with the wood") has no special sign, only the direction "col legno," which has to be written out at the beginning of the passage where the effect is wanted. The col legno itself — tapping the strings with the stick of the bow instead of bowing them — can be combined with the glissando, with the tremolo, and with harmonics — all very good orchestral effects. The instruction for returning to normal bowing, "modo ord." (modo ordinario), must always be written out.

The **sul ponticello** ("near the bridge") effect, for which, once again, there is no special mark, is a nasal, metallic sound produced by bowing very close to the bridge. After the "sul pont." section it is necessary to write out the direction for using the normal position: modo ord.

Sul tasto, meaning "on the fingerboard," is a flute-like effect, produced by bowing very slightly over the fingerboard. This is a fine effect for playing sustained passages or slow notes. It has no special sign other than the written-out direction, "sul tasto." After the section so played the direction for using the normal position of the bow, modo ord., must be written out.

The strings of the instruments are **numbered** from the highest to the lowest by Roman numerals (I, II, III, IV; see page 27). If a passage or section is to be played on a specific string (e.g. "sul D" on the violin), then it is marked in modern notation with the number of the string:

Con sordino (or plural: sordini, both abbr. "sord.") means "with the mute." This well-known and often used effect sounds best on the violin and viola, although it is sometimes required on the 'cellos and double basses too. It is very effective at any dynamic grade. The effect is produced by a small clamp, placed on the bridge of the instrument. If the sordino is required it is necessary to leave *time* (about 10 seconds) for the player to prepare his instrument. The termination of the effect is always marked with the words "Senza sordino" or "Senza sord."

III
Signs Used in Notation of Wind Music

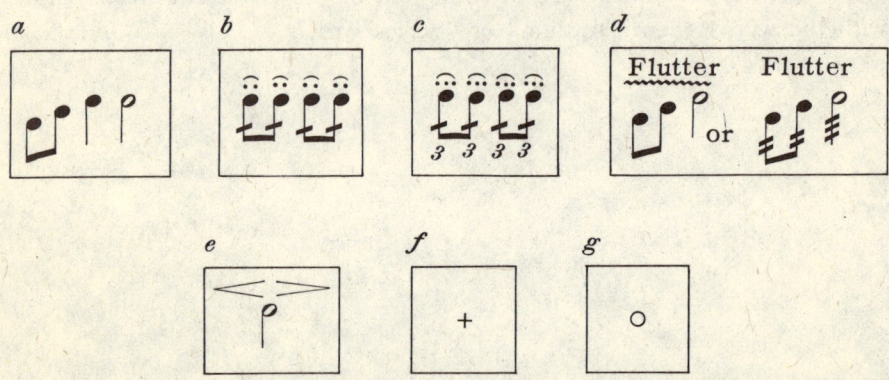

In wind instruments the tongue is used as a means of articulation much as the bow is used in the strings. **Tonguing** is a method of separating the tones from one another. There are three types of tongued articulation:

Single tonguing (t-t-t-t . . .)

Double tonguing (t-k / t-k / t-k . . .)

Triple tonguing (t-k-t / t-k-t / t-k-t . . .)

Single tonguing (under a) above) is the most common and has no special sign. It is only the separation of one note from another so long as the passage is not too fast to permit its use.

When the notes become too rapid **double tonguing** and **triple tonguing** are employed. They are mostly used in quick passages for double (b) and triple (c) repetition of notes. The correct notation and effect of these:

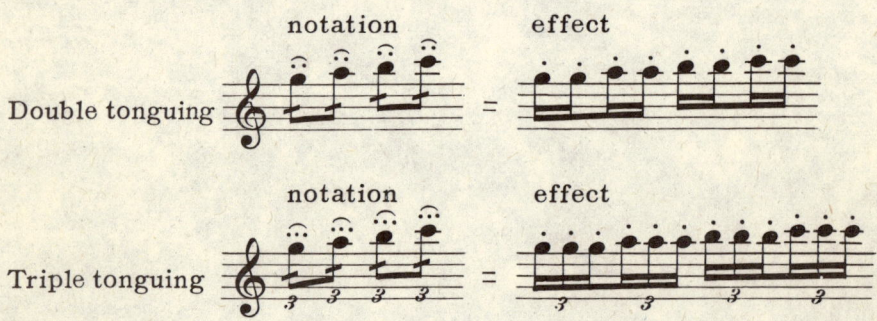

There is also a special effect known as **flutter-tonguing** (d) which is indicated in two ways: by a continuous horizontal wavy line above the notes with the direction "flutter," or by tremolo notes with the indication "flutter" above them:

This is a harsh rolling effect which sounds very much like drrrrr. When properly used on single notes or in passages, it can be a very effective orchestral device.

The **messa di voce,** i.e. "placing the voice" (see e) above), an ornament employed by singers in the 18th century, is used in contemporary music, mostly in wind parts. The mark indicates a fairly quick crescendo of a sustained note from p to $f\!f$ followed immediately by a quick decrescendo back to p. The whole effect is always as long as the value of the note.

The sign at f) above indicates **stopped** tones on the **horn.** The cross is either placed over each note or prolonged by a dotted line:

The sign at g) above indicates **open** (i.e. normal) playing on the horn to cancel the cross.

Con sord. in horns, trumpets and trombones (rarely in tuba parts) indicates the use of one of the mutes. The type of mute is always indicated by name.

The direction is followed until the indication for open playing appears: **senza sord.** (without mute), or simply: **open.**

IV
Signs Used in Notation for Percussion Instruments

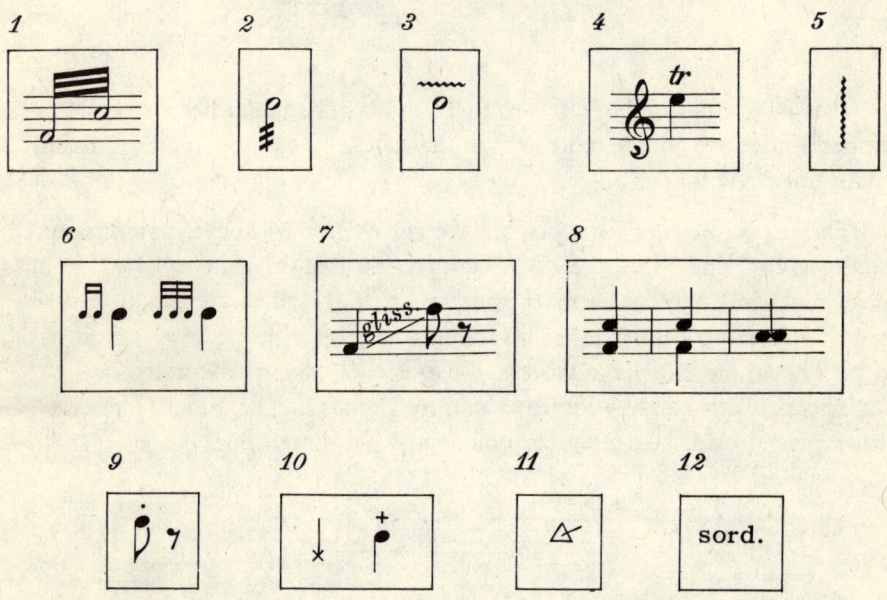

Timpani. — Notation always in bass clef. No key signature; the accidentals are to be written out each time. For range see page 29.

Normal method of playing: striking with two sticks whose knobs are covered with felt.

Special effects: TREMOLO (1). For correct notation see page 11.
ROLL (2)
WITH TWO STICKS AT THE SAME TIME (8)
SORD. or COPERTO (12), indicating the use of sponge-headed sticks as mutes.
SECCO or SUFFOCATO (9) — i.e. dry, muffled.
GLISSANDO (7)

Glockenspiel. — Notation in violin clef. Key signature necessary. For range see page 29.

Normal method of playing if not an instrument with a keyboard: striking with two small wooden or metal hammers.

No special effects.

Xylophone. — Notation in violin clef. Key signature necessary. For range see page 29.

Normal method of playing if not an instrument with a keyboard: striking with two light wooden hammers.

Special effects: TREMOLO (1). For correct notation see page 51.
GLISSANDO (7)
TRILL (4), played like a tremolo.

Celesta. — Notation in violin and bass clefs on a great staff. Key signature necessary. For range see page 30.

Normal method of playing: on a keyboard.

Special effects: AREPEGGIO (5). For notation see page 19.
GLISSANDO (7)
TREMOLO (1). For correct notation see page 51.

Vibraphone. — Notation in violin clef on a single or a great staff. Key signature necessary.

Normal method of playing: striking with two or more (for chords) sticks whose knobs are covered with hard felt.

Special effects: ARPEGGIO (5), slow execution only.
GLISSANDO (7), with wooden sticks.

Triangle. — Notation without clef and key signature on a single line. The instrument is indicated by the sign at 11 above.

Normal method of playing: striking with a short metal bar.

Special effects: TREMOLO (3)
SORD. (12) — mute: by touching the instrument with one hand and at the same time striking with the metal stick in the other.

Snare and **Tenor Drums.** — No clef and key signature used. Notation on a single line.

Normal method of playing: striking or rolling with two light wooden sticks.

Special effects: SECCO or SUFFOCATO (9) — i.e. dry, muffled.
SORD. (12) — mute: by placing a cloth over the parchment, or by loosening the snares.
LONG ROLLS (3)
SHORT ROLLS (6)

Bass drum. — No clef and key signature. Notation on a single line.

Normal method of playing: striking with a single or double-headed heavy wooden or hard felt stick or mallet.

Special effects: ROLL (3), with a double-headed stick.
STRIKING BOTH SIDES AT THE SAME TIME (8)
TREMOLO (2), usually with two hard timpani sticks.
SECCO or SUFFOCATO (9) — i.e. dry, muffled.

Cymbals. — No clef and key signature. Notation on a single line.

Normal method of playing: striking the two brass plates together.

Special effects: RUBBED TOGETHER (3)
TREMOLO (2) — quick, short strokes on a single plate with timpani sticks. The effect could be a tremendous crescendo.
SUFFOCATO (9) — i.e. immediately muffled.
STRUCK TOGETHER (10), indicating the normal use after a special effect.

Tambourine. — No clef and key signature. Notation on a single line.

Normal method of playing: striking the skin with the knuckles.

Special effects: SHAKING ONLY (3)
TREMOLO (2) — rubbing the thumb on the skin, which produces a tremolo of the jingles.

Gong. — No clef and key signature. Notation on a single line.

Normal method of playing: striking with a heavy bass-drum stick.

Special effects: TREMOLO (2) — continuous rapid strokes with two hard timpani sticks.
SECCO (9) — one short stroke immediately muffled.

V
Signs Commonly Used in Harp, Piano, and Organ Music

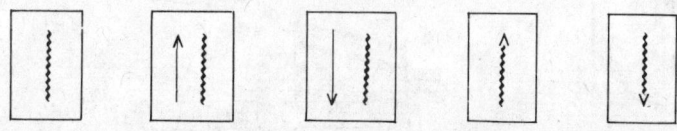

The vertical wavy line indicates **arpeggio;** the notes of the chord (or sometimes just an interval) so marked are to be played one after the other instead of simultaneously. If not otherwise indicated, the execution of an arpeggio always starts with the lowest note of the chord. Modern composers often require the execution of the arpeggio in reverse. The reversed arpeggio starts with the upper note of the chord and ends with the lowest.

The following arpeggio marks are now used:

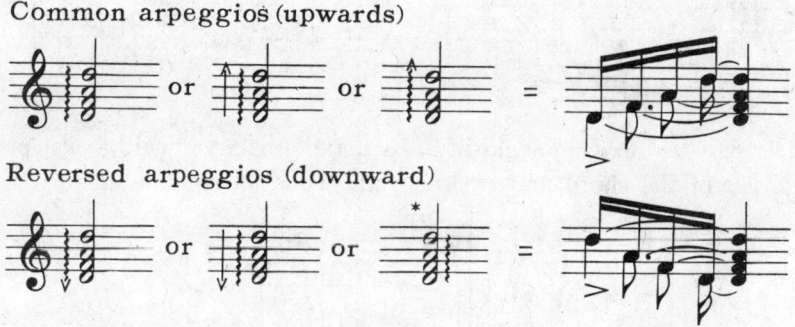

(The sign for reversed arpeggio marked * is used only by Bartók and is not the best.)

In the great staff arpeggios are written in two ways. If the wavy line is broken between the two staves, the arpeggio is simultaneous in both hands:

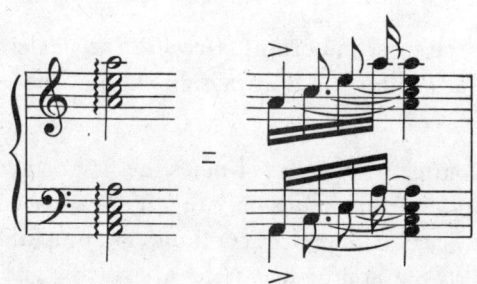

If the wavy line is not broken and goes across the whole great staff, all the notes of the chord must be played in succession from the lowest to the highest (or from highest to lowest according to the indication):

An arpeggio can be done in both directions at the same time:

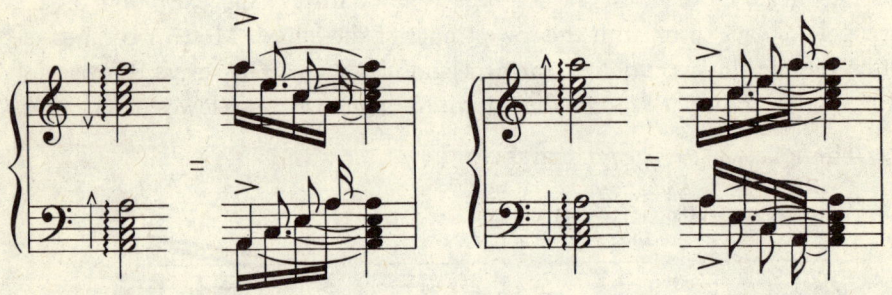

The sign for **non arpeggio** in **harp** notation is a vertical bracket placed to the left of the chord and enclosing all of its notes:

This example also shows the sign for the harp-effect **Let vibrate**: this is the short horizontal slur starting on each note of the chord.

Perhaps one of the most important effects in the modern orchestra is the **harp glissando.** The sign for this is always an oblique line between two noteheads.

In the case of complex sequences of notes the first octave of the glissando is usually written out, and thereafter only the sign leading to the top point of the glissando is necessary. If the effect continues in an up and down glissando (or vice versa) the lowest and highest notes are usually given and connected by the sign. In addition, the situation of the pedals is usually marked at the same time, as is shown below (glissando with enharmonic doublings):

In the case of chord (or interval) glissandos each note of the starting chord (interval) is connected with a line to the last chord of the glissando:

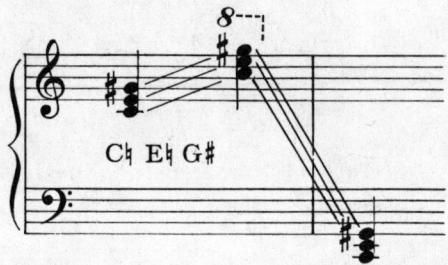

Of course it is almost impossible to show all the variants of the harp glissando effect. Only the most common methods of marking are given here, but they show the principles of marking.

The sign mostly used to indicate **harmonics on the harp** is the mark ° *above* the note (a). It is also used in chords, in which case each note has to have the sign as shown below (b):

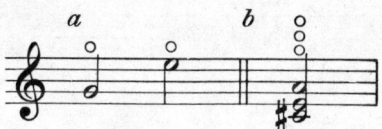

In piano notation the mark of glissando is the same oblique line, connecting the starting and ending note of the effect, with the abbreviation "gliss." above it.

The marks for indicating **pedaling in piano music:**

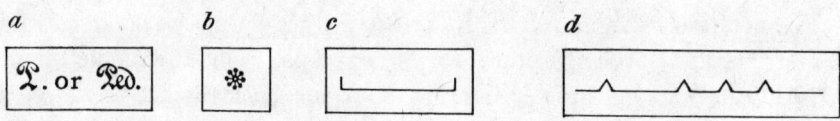

All these indicate the use of the **damper-pedal** only. The first two (a) indicate the depressing of the damper-pedal and the large asterisk (b) indicates its release. These two marks are the most common. The hook (c) marks the length of the effect. The last (d) indicates interrupted or changing pedaling, i.e. after the damper-pedal is held down for a while (during the horizontal sections of the mark) it is quickly released and immediately depressed again (wedges). The formation of the mark depends always on the required changing effect.

The mark for using the left ("soft") pedal on the piano is **una corda,** and for releasing it **tre corde.**

There are two marks in **organ music** indicating the "footing" of the pedal part:

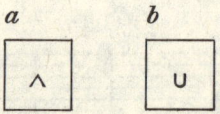

The first mark (a) indicates **toe,** the second (b) **heel.** Both marks written *above* the notes indicate the use of the *right* foot. Written *under* the notes, they indicate the *left* foot:

A change of toe and heel on relatively long notes is indicated by both signs connected with a slur:

A change of foot is indicated by placing the mark above and below the note at the same time:

The notation of organ music always needs three lines: the great staff for the manuals, and one staff below it for the pedal part. Notating the left hand and the pedal on the same staff must be avoided, because it often causes mistakes.

VI
The Range of Musical Instruments and the Human Voice

The nomenclature is given in this sequence: English, Italian, French, and German. Only the most common abbreviations are given.

A. WOODWINDS
(For special notation see page 14.)

Piccolo	Flauto piccolo	Petite flûte	Kleine Flöte
(Picc.)	or Ottavino	(p^{te} fl.)	(Kl. Fl.)
	(picc.)		

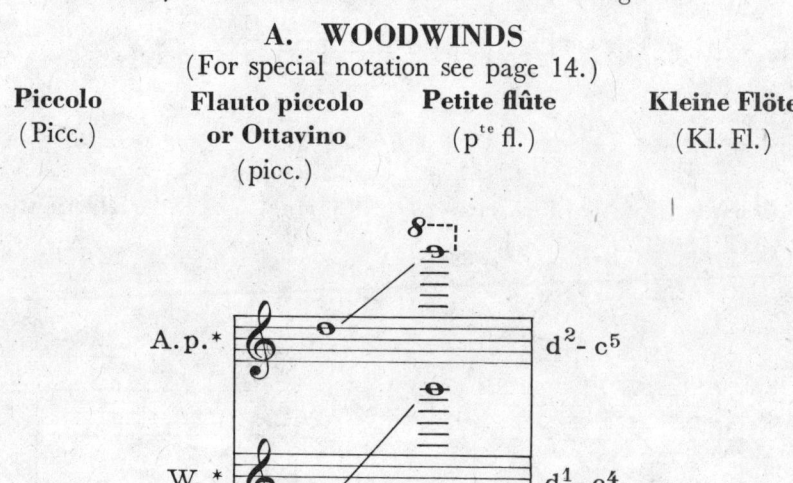

A.p.* d^2- c^5

W.* d^1- c^4

*A. p. for Actual pitch; W. for Written pitch.

Flute	Flauto or	Grande flûte	Grosse Flöte
(Fl.)	Flauto grande	(G^{de} fl.)	(Gr. Fl. or Fl.)
	(Fl., or Fl. gr.)		

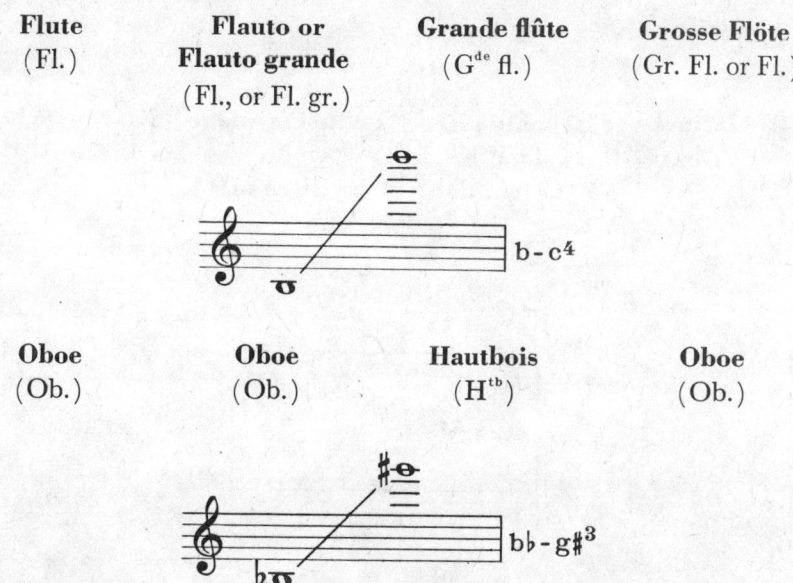

b- c^4

| Oboe | Oboe | Hautbois | Oboe |
| (Ob.) | (Ob.) | (H^{tb}) | (Ob.) |

b♭- g♯^{3}

English Horn **Corno inglese** **Cor anglais** **Englisch Horn**
(Eng. Hn.)   (Cor. ingl.)   (Cor. ang.)   (Engl. Hr. or E. H.)

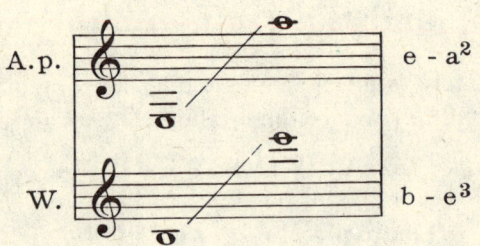

A.p. e - a²
W. b - e³

Clarinet **Clarinetto** **Clarinette** **Klarinette**
(Cl.)   (Cl.)   (Cl.)   (Kl.)

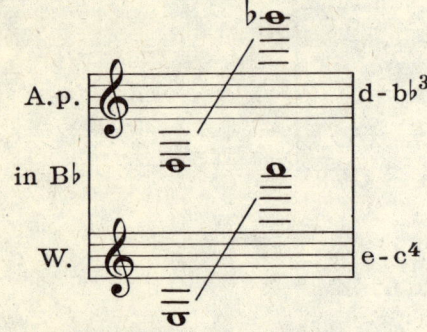

A.p. in B♭ d - b♭³
W. e - c⁴

A.p. in A c♯ - a³
W. e - c⁴

E♭ Clarinet **Clarinetto piccolo in Mi♭** **Petite Clarinette en Mi♭** **Klarinette in Es**
(E♭ Cl.)   (Cl. in Mi♭)   (pᵗᵉ Cl. en Mi♭)   (Es-Kl.)

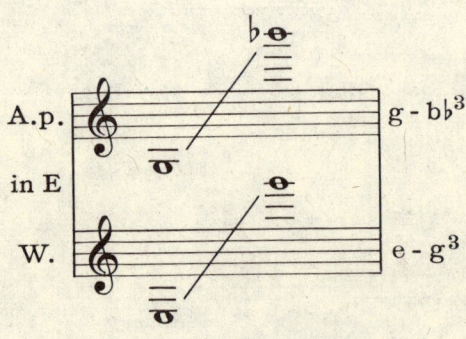

A.p. in E g - b♭³
W. e - g³

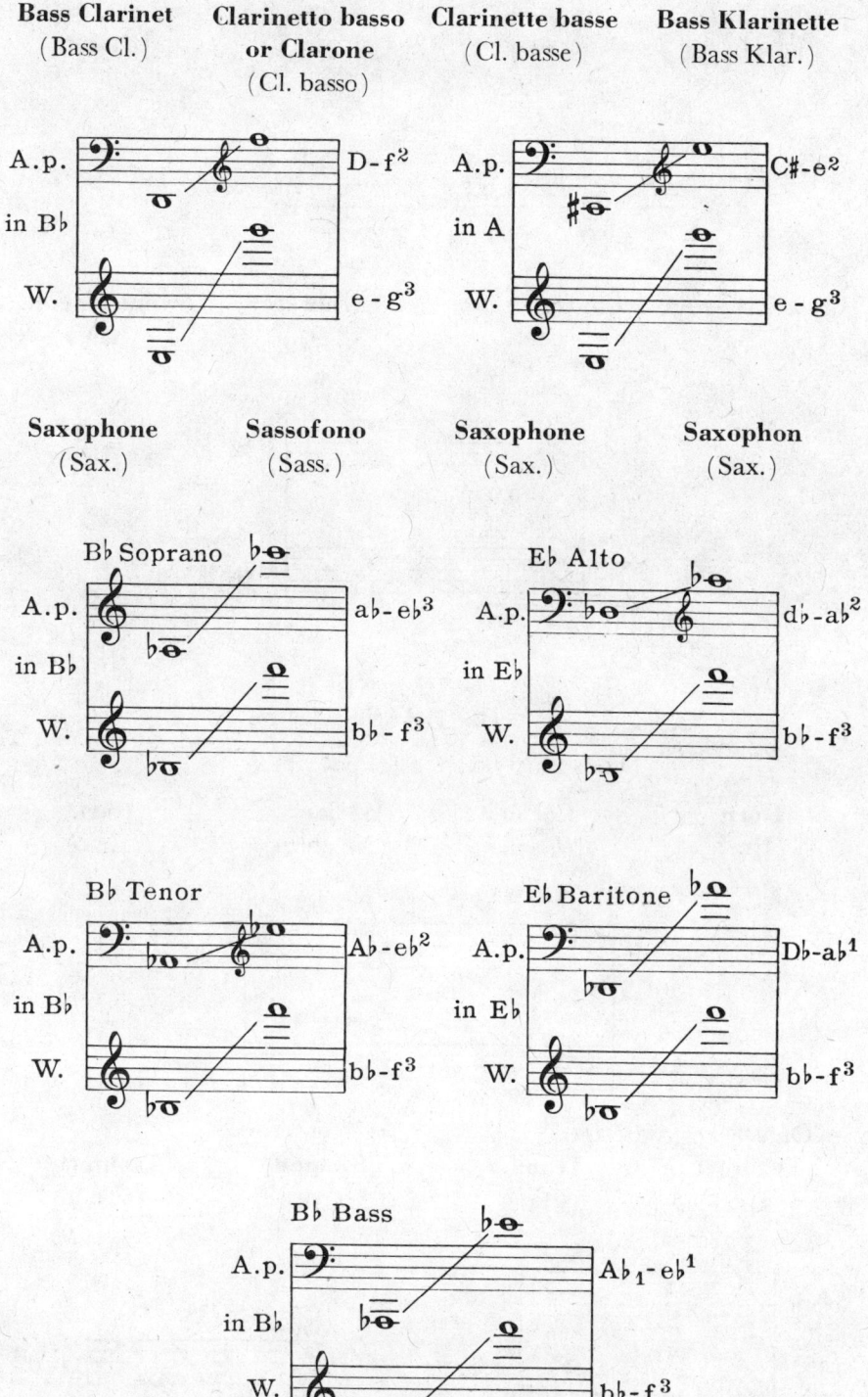

26

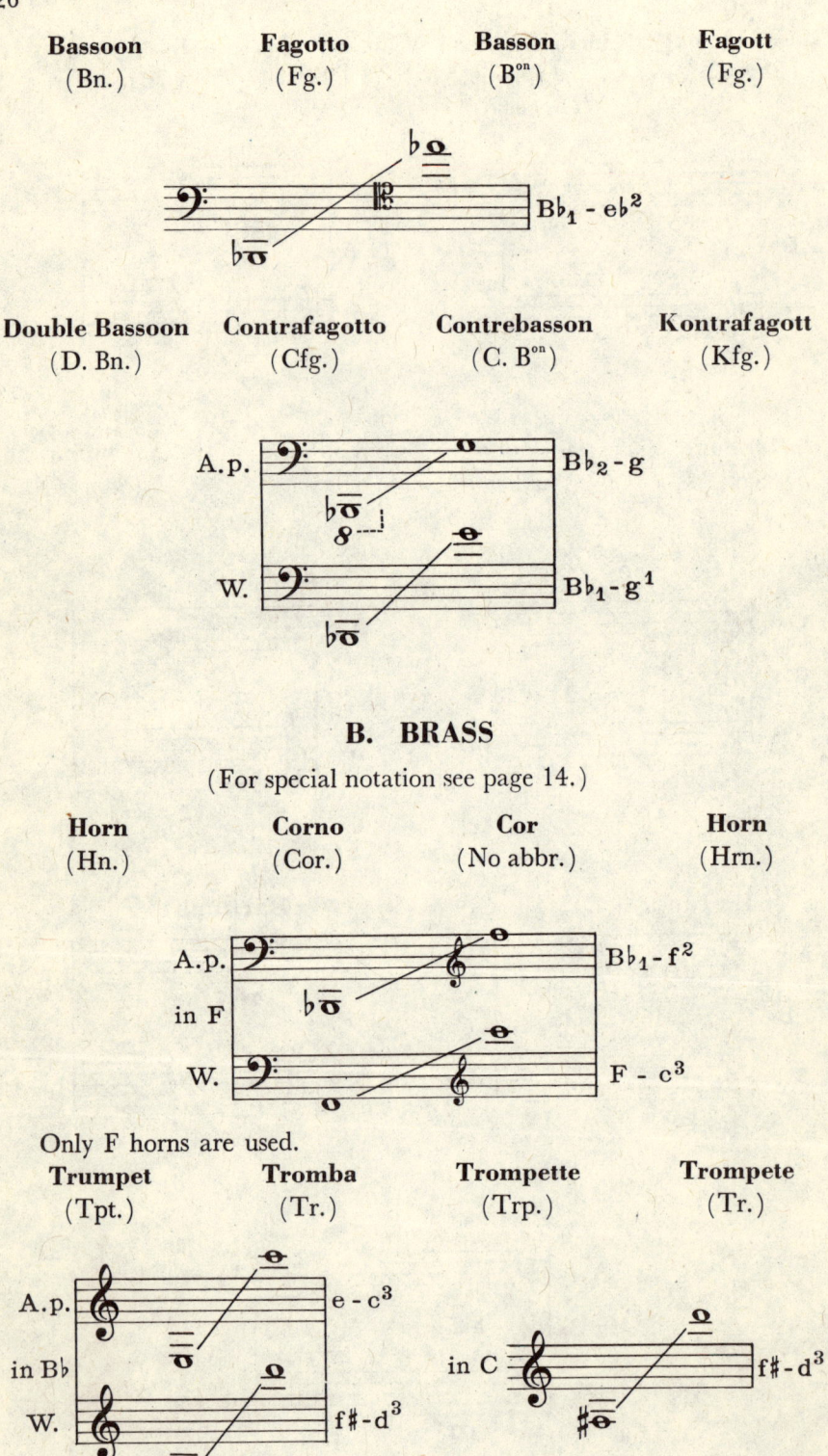

Bassoon	Fagotto	Basson	Fagott
(Bn.)	(Fg.)	(B^{on})	(Fg.)

$Bb_1 - eb^2$

Double Bassoon	Contrafagotto	Contrebasson	Kontrafagott
(D. Bn.)	(Cfg.)	(C. B^{on})	(Kfg.)

A.p. $Bb_2 - g$

W. $Bb_1 - g^1$

B. BRASS
(For special notation see page 14.)

Horn	Corno	Cor	Horn
(Hn.)	(Cor.)	(No abbr.)	(Hrn.)

A.p. in F $Bb_1 - f^2$

W. $F - c^3$

Only F horns are used.

Trumpet	Tromba	Trompette	Trompete
(Tpt.)	(Tr.)	(Trp.)	(Tr.)

A.p. in Bb $e - c^3$

W. $f\#-d^3$

in C $f\#-d^3$

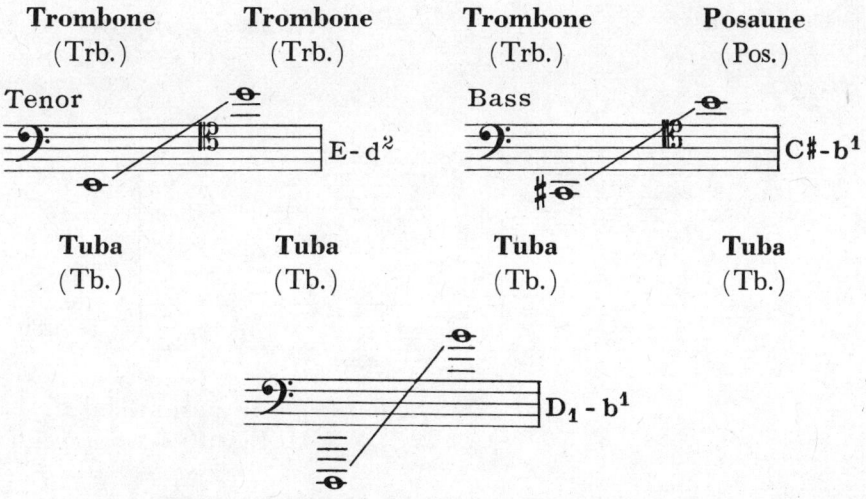

C. STRINGS

(For bowing and special notation see page 8.)

Extreme range in parentheses.

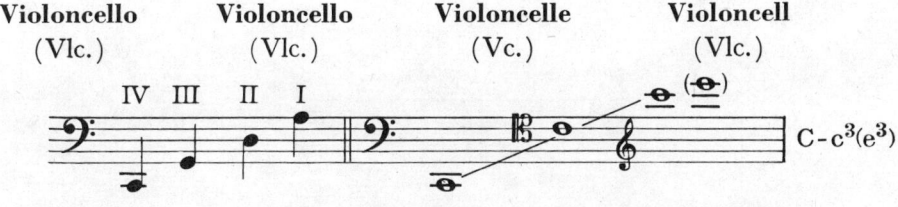

Extreme range in parentheses.

Double Bass	Contrabasso	Contrebasse	Kontrabass
(D. B.)	(Cb.)	(Cb.)	(Kbass.)

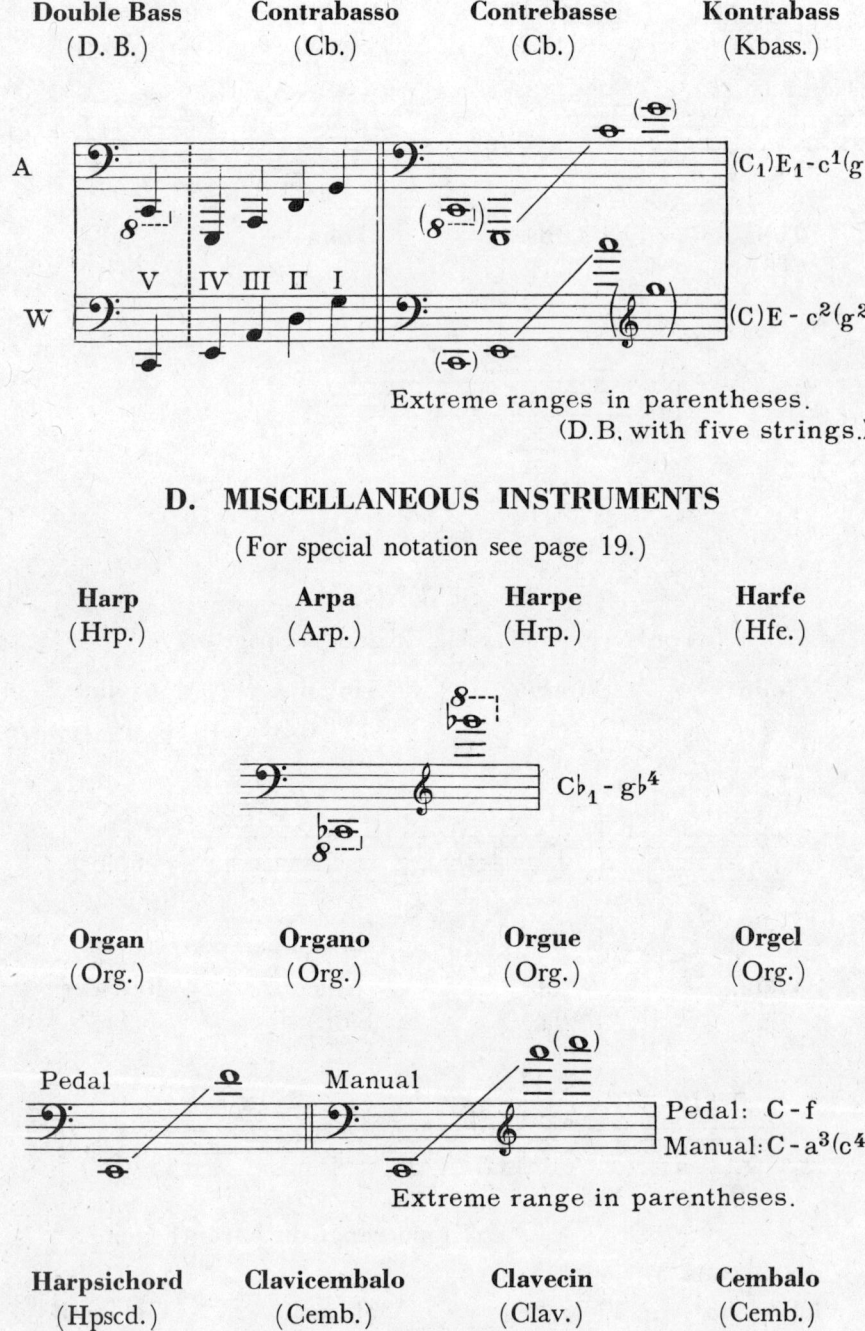

Extreme ranges in parentheses.
(D.B. with five strings.)

D. MISCELLANEOUS INSTRUMENTS

(For special notation see page 19.)

Harp	Arpa	Harpe	Harfe
(Hrp.)	(Arp.)	(Hrp.)	(Hfe.)

$Cb_1 - gb^4$

Organ	Organo	Orgue	Orgel
(Org.)	(Org.)	(Org.)	(Org.)

Pedal: C-f
Manual: $C - a^3 (c^4)$

Extreme range in parentheses.

Harpsichord	Clavicembalo	Clavecin	Cembalo
(Hpscd.)	(Cemb.)	(Clav.)	(Cemb.)

$A_1 - c^3 (g^3)$

E. PERCUSSIONS OF DEFINITE PITCH
(For special notation see page 16.)

Timpani	Timpani	Timbales	Pauken
(Timp., K. Dr.)	(Timp.)	(Timb.)	(P. K.)

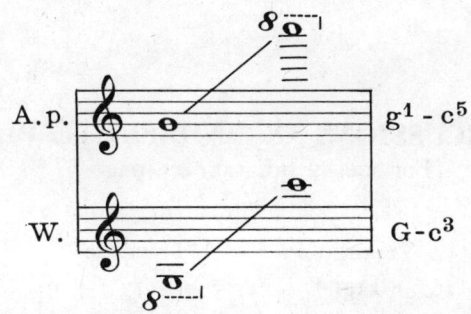
D - a

Glockenspiel	Campanelli	Carillon	Glockenspiel
(Glsp.)	(Cmpli.)	(Car.)	(Glsp.)

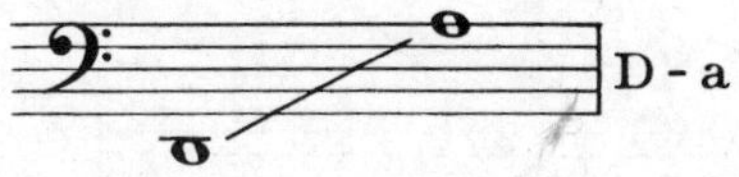

A.p. $g^1 - c^5$

W. $G - c^3$

Xylophone	Silofono	Xylophone	Xylophon
(Xyl.)	(Sil.)	(Xyl.)	(Xyl.)

$g - c^4$

Vibraphone	Vibrafono	Vibraphone	Vibraphon
(Vib.)	(Vibraf.)	(Vibraph.)	(Vibraph.)

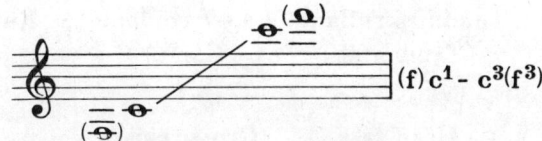
(f) $c^1 - c^3(f^3)$

Extreme ranges in parentheses.

| Celesta | Celesta | Celeste | Celeste |
| (Cel.) | (Cel.) | (Cel.) | (Cel.) |

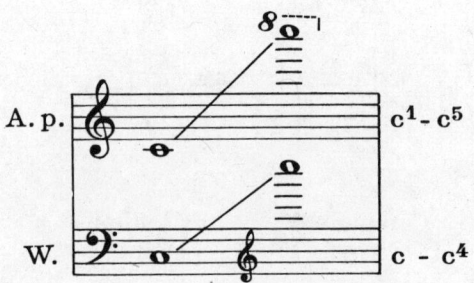

A. p. $c^1 - c^5$

W. $c - c^4$

F. PERCUSSIONS OF INDEFINITE PITCH
(For special notation see page 17.)

Triangle	Triangolo	Triangle	Triangel
(Trgl.)	(Trgl.)	(Trg.)	(Trgl.)
Cymbals	Piatti	Cymbales	Becken
(Cymb.)	(Ptti.)	(Cymb.)	(Beck.)
Tambourine	Tamburello Basco	Tambour de Basque	Schellentrommel
(Tamb.)	(Tbr. B.)	(Tamb. de B.)	(Schtr.)
Gong	Gong	Gong	Gong
(G.)	(G.)	(G.)	(G.)
Snare Drum	Tamburo	Caisse claire	Kleine Trommel
(Sn. Dr.)	(Tamb.)	(Caisse)	(Kl. Tr.)
Tenor Drum	Tamburo rullante	Caisse roulante	Rührtrommel
(Ten. Dr.)	(Tamb. rull.)	(C. roul.)	(Rtr.)
Bass Drum	Gran casa	Grosse caisse	Grosse Trommel
(B. Dr.)	(Gr. c.)	(Gr. c.)	(Gr. Tr.)

G. MIXED CHORUSES

Soprano	Sopran	Soprano	Soprano
(S.)	(S.)	(S.)	(S.)
Alto	Alto	Contralto	Alt
(A.)	(A.)	(Cont.)	(A.)
Tenor	Tenore	Ténor	Tenor
(T.)	(T.)	(T.)	(T.)
Bass	Basso	Basse	Bass
(B.)	(B.)	(B.)	(B.)

Adult or professional singers:

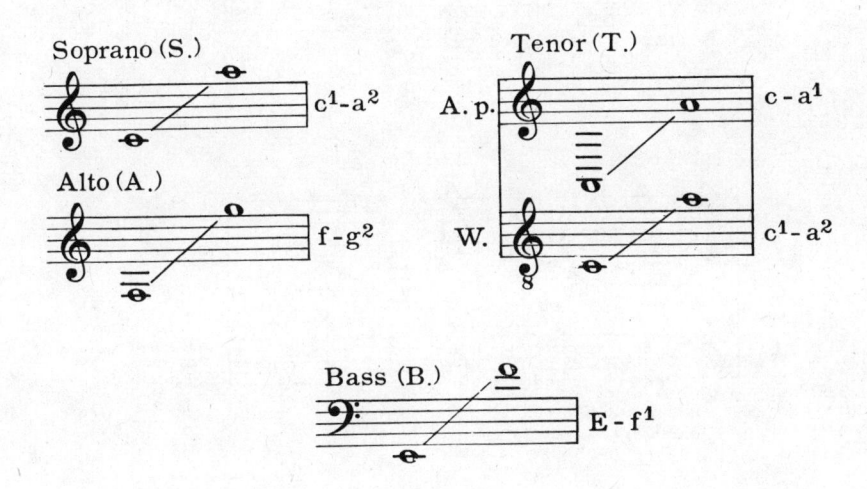

Soprano (S.) $c^1 - a^2$

Tenor (T.)   A.p. $c - a^1$

Alto (A.) $f - g^2$

W. $c^1 - a^2$

Bass (B.) $E - f^1$

Senior high school mixed chorus (with a high degree of safety):

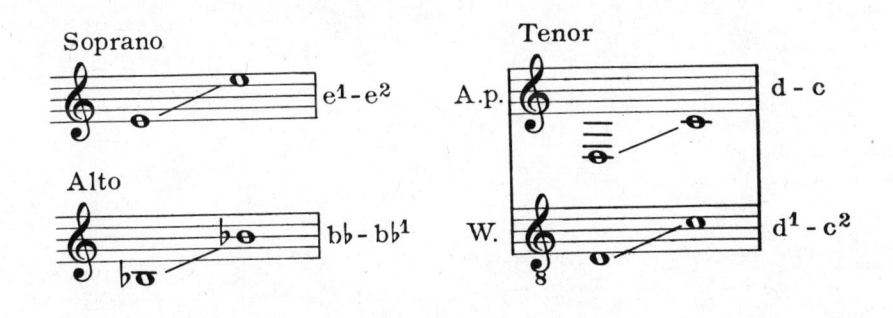

Soprano $e^1 - e^2$

Tenor   A.p. $d - c$

Alto $b\flat - b\flat^1$

W. $d^1 - c^2$

Bass $B\flat - b\flat$

The extreme range for high school voice-parts:

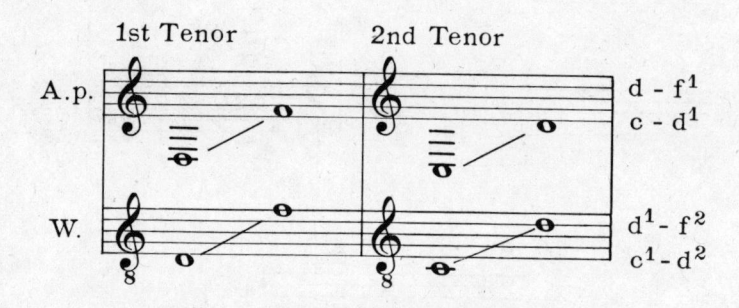

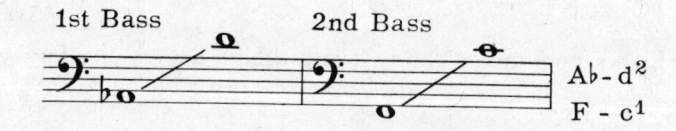

1st Soprano   2nd Soprano $d^1 - a^2$
                                          $c^1 - f^2$

1st Alto   2nd Alto $b\flat - d^2$
                                $a\flat - c^2$

A.p.   1st Tenor   2nd Tenor $d - f^1$
                                        $c - d^1$

W. $d^1 - f^2$
                                        $c^1 - d^2$

1st Bass   2nd Bass $A\flat - d^2$
                                $F - c^1$

VII
The Technique of Correct Modern Musical Notation

§ 1. Up to and including the second space of the staff the stems of the notes go upward on the *right side* of the note-head. From the third line on up, they are drawn downward on the *left side* of the head.

§ 2. The third line is "neutral." A note there usually has the stem drawn downward but it could also be drawn upward. Likewise with notes equally distant from it if they are on the same stem:

§ 3. In two-part notation when both parts are written on one staff, the stems of the upper part are drawn upward, the stems of the lower part downward, regardless of the position on the staff. The rests of the individual parts are indicated where they replace notes, and exactly on the same level.

§ 4. In groups of notes connected by beams the location of the majority of notes above or below the "neutral" line determines whether the stems should be drawn upward or down.

§ 5. The direction of the beam generally follows the direction of the rising or falling notes (see ex. above). Beams of figures that begin and end with the same note or outline the same interval, however, should be horizontal:

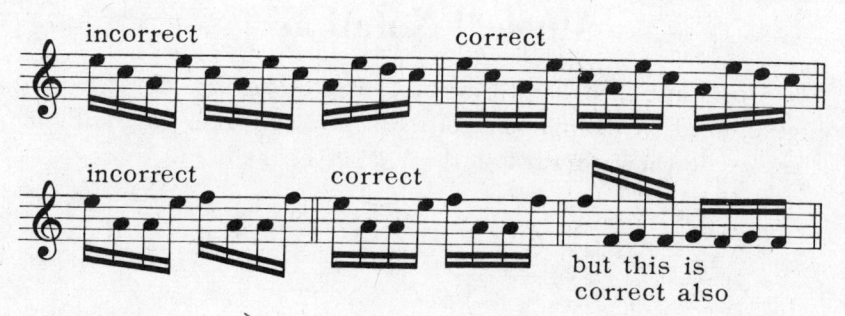

incorrect   correct

incorrect   correct

but this is
correct also

In vocal part notation (in scores or individual parts) flags are no longer used exclusively, as they were formerly; the values are expressed by beams. Exceptions to use of beams are only justified in case of a new musical idea or on account of the prosody. Notes that do not have separate syllables (a so-called melisma) usually have a slur above them (see page 3). Another exception is in popular music, where the old-fashioned notation with flags in the voice-part is still often used.

§ 6. Stems for chords also depend on the "neutral" line: the guide being the direction of stem of the majority of the notes (see § 4).

§ 7. When the notes of a chord are so crowded that they cannot be written or printed directly above each other, the direction of the stem is especially important. The note that has to be placed beside another one in the chord is called a "suspended" note. The rule for such cases is that the *lower* neighboring note is *always* placed to the left of the stem, the higher to the right. For example, of the five different notations of the three notes below, only the one framed is correct:

because the direction of the stems is determined by the majority of the notes, they are consequently on the proper side, and the lower of the neighboring notes is on the left side. Other examples:

The rule remains the same when leger lines are needed. The same principle applies for chords of whole notes. They are to be written as if with a stem. However since they do not have a stem we can notate the chords two ways:

Of the two b) is better because a downward stem is preferable, the majority of the notes being above the 3rd line. If a moving part is added to this group, the stems of the new part would be drawn in the opposite direction (see § 3):

This example also shows that the first note of such a part moving among notes of a chord has its stem placed very close to that of the chord. They are actually sounded together. The second measure proves that a dotted note cannot be placed before a whole note, because the prolonging dot could hardly be appropriately placed, and the notation pattern would be poor (try it!). An undotted note so placed might be acceptable:

§ 8. Expression marks of notes on a single stem are written out only once, on the level opposite the direction of the stem, close to the note-heads. In these cases the marks apply to *all the notes* on the stem. Whenever possible, dynamic indications are put *below* the staff.

In vocal parts, these rules cannot always be applied, because of possible confusion with the words. In such cases the marks are generally placed on the level *opposite the text*. Care must be exercised to make it very clear where the marks belong. It should not be possible to apply them to another part.

§ 9. The dynamic marks of each part should be together and not separated. E.g. the notation in the example below is incorrect because

the < and "cresc." are above, instead of below, between the beginning and terminating dynamic marks. The above example correctly written:

§ 10. The various indications must be put together carefully. The poor construction of the example below is taken from a printed orchestral part:

Here, the "trem." and the "pointe d'archet" belong together, meaning "tremolo with the point of the bow." The proper placing of such a crowded note pattern is difficult because generally there is little space. In part-writing this should have been put together like this:

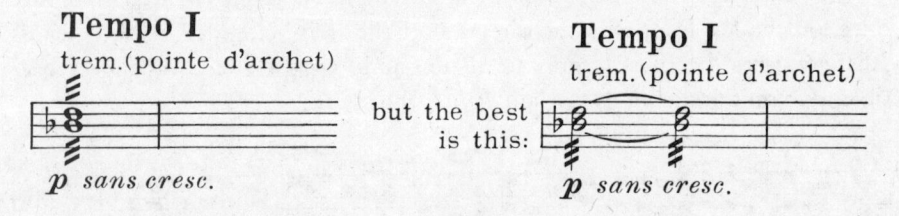

but the best is this:

§ 11. In single part notation, expression marks, tenutos, staccatos, accents, etc. as well as their combined forms should be close to the noteheads following their direction on the staff:

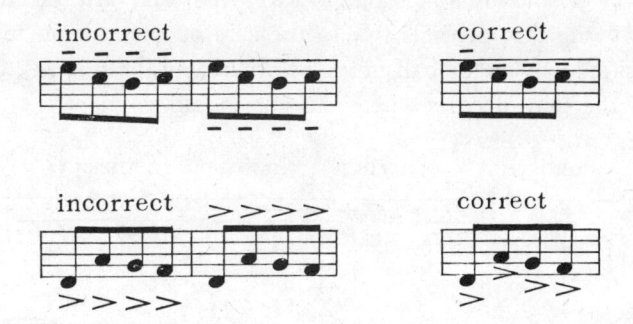

§ 12. In cases where "suspended" notes occur in chords, the expression marks are put above (or below) those notes of the chord which influence the direction of the stem. Consequently not above the stem, or between notes of the chord, or above the "suspended" note:

§ 13. Slurs have various functions (see page 2). The tie should almost touch the note-heads:

Above a tie there may also be a slur, for phrasing or legato, which cannot be placed well unless the tie is in its proper position:

§ 14. Slurs at the beginning of a line, which connect notes to the previous one, should be short and nearly horizontal if they end on the line's first note:

§ 15. Ties in monophonic (single-part) material always curve in the direction *opposite* that of the stem. In the case of whole notes, the slurs are drawn the same way as for half notes, or other notes with stems, because the direction of the stem decides where the slur should be placed:

§ 16. Slurs are generally placed at the heads of notes. In cases where the figure or melody has stems changing between upward and down, the slur is placed above, even though there may be *only one stem going downward* in the group below it:

When two parts on the same stem are legato, the slur must not be put between the heads of repeated notes on the same pitch, because it would then become a tie (a). In such a case the placing of the slur is decided in exception to the rule (b):

§ 17. When two curved lines are used together, one as a tie and the other as a slur (see § 13, Ex. 2), they are placed as follows:

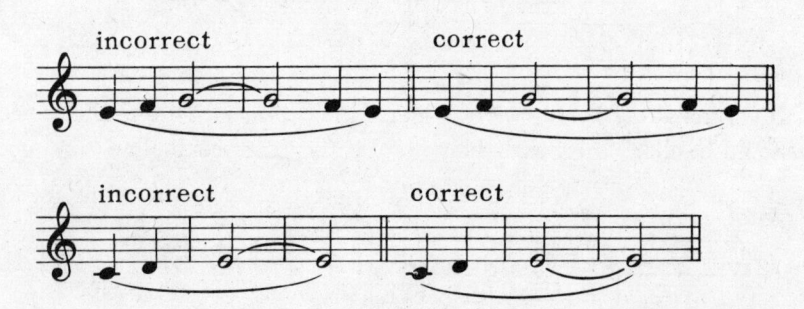

§ 18. Legatos for chords are generally marked with a single slur (a) as though they were a single part. Other expression marks also need only be written out once. Tied notes in a chord have the ties placed as shown in b).

§ 19. In legato chords we only use more than one slur if the others signify ties (held notes). At such times, the slurs curve in opposite directions if the notes are of quarter-note or longer values:

§ 20. Tied notes in beamed chords have their slurs curve away from the beam (a); however if there is also a legato mark on the chord, the tie (inner slur) curves towards the beam, the other being in the opposite direction (b):

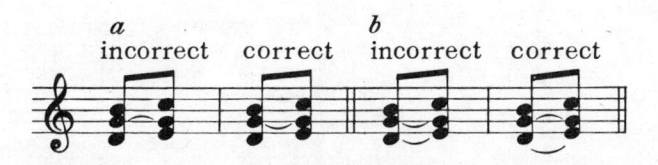

§ 21. If a single note has two stems, it gets two slurs when with its next step it goes in two different directions although on the same stem:

§ 22. Some examples of where to put expression marks when slurs are used also:

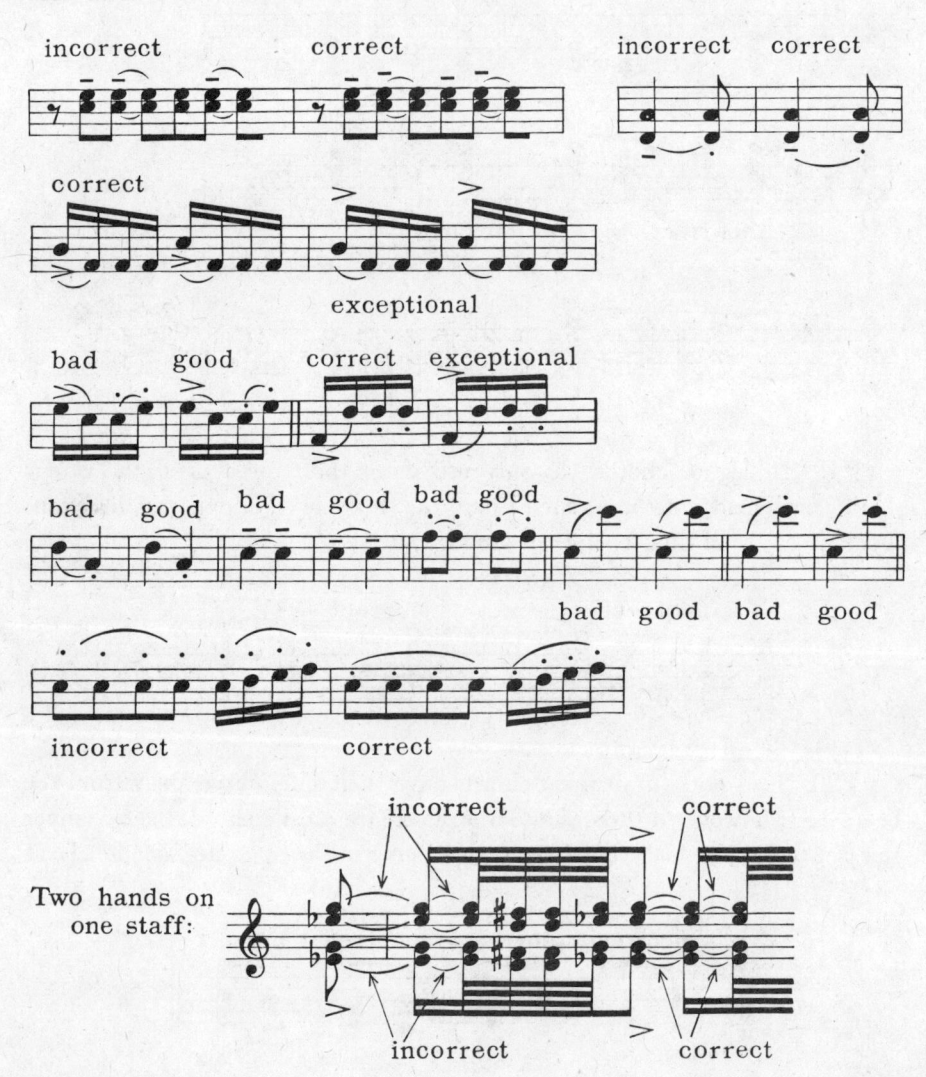

Two hands on one staff:

§ 23. Notes on different stems but on the same staff (two-part notation) have separate dynamic marks, placed on the outer sides. They are next to the stems and not to the note-heads:

§ 24. The rests — except half and whole rests — do not have a fixed place on the staff. They are usually put in the middle of the staff, but if necessary they may stand above or below the staff also. The whole rest generally *hangs* down from the fourth line (a), the half *lies* on the third (b). If it is necessary to use these rests above or below the staff, they hang or lie always on a leger line (c):

§ 25. If two or more parts on one staff within the same measure all pause together for the same length of time, the appropriate rest need be written only once. Consequently, the first example below is wrong, the second right. In case one part has a pause for a whole bar, a whole rest is put in the middle of the bar, whatever the time signature.

In contrast to this rest, note-heads should never be written in the center of a measure. Notes and rests — with the exception mentioned above — are always put in the part of measure where they actually sound or begin. For a rest lasting through several bars in orchestral or choral parts the sign is abbreviated. It becomes a thick, horizontal line closed at both ends, above which is written the number of bars covered by the rest:

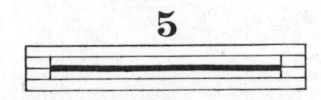

§ 26. Slurs should reach precisely from note-head to note-head, or stem to stem (see § 13). Care must be exercised; carelessly drawn slurs often cause confusion.

§ 27. If a work is notated on several staves, special care must be taken that dynamic marks are correctly placed. This applies especially to full scores. Dynamic marks always apply to the staff to which they are *closest:*

§ 28. When dynamic marks are placed halfway between two staves, they apply to *both* staves:

§ 29. When there are several parts with different metrical values, it is very important that the note values be correctly spaced vertically. Correct assignment of space helps make the reading of notes easier. Careful spacing is particularly important in full scores. Care should be taken that the noteheads, not their stems, be in line vertically.

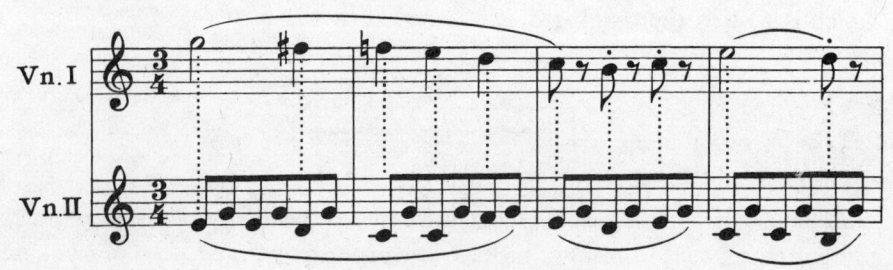

§ 30. Sudden dynamic changes should be made noticeable in the note patterns also. Especially in continuous passages of equal note values:

old notation

modern notation

Such emphasis is also useful in separating phrases:

old notation

better

§ 31. There are three ways to indicate change of key signature during the course of a piece. The old method of doing this was, after a double barline, to cancel first the previous key signature — completely or partially — by naturals, then to write in the new key signature:

This method, although often used, is not the best because it sometimes makes the new key signature crowded.

A better way is to place the naturals that cancel the old signature before the double barline, and after it the new one. This is more modern than the first method:

The best and most modern way is a third one: it is not necessary to cancel by naturals the affected notes of the previous signature, because the indication of the new key signature is completely sufficient:

There is only one time when the previous signature must be cancelled after a double barline, and that is when the new key is C major or A minor:

Repeat signs are not barlines, although they often come together with the barlines. The example below shows where repeat signs have been placed in case of simultaneous change of key and time signature:

incorrect   correct

§ 32. Temporary accidentals are valid throughout the measure in which they occur. Generally they do not need a natural sign to cancel them in the next measure. Within the measure the permanent accidental noted at the beginning of the staff (key signature) is written out again in parentheses if the same note is altered in another part:

§ 33. With two parts on a single staff, accidentals must be written out when they occur for each of the parts. However, if the several parts are played by a single player (organ, piano, etc.), the accidentals are only written once:

OBOE I   PIANO

OBOE II

§ 34. If an altered note is tied over to the following measure, at the end of the tie and beginning of the bar the accidental generally is not written out again (although certain modern publications follow this practice), but if the same altered tone is repeated without a preceding tie, the alteration must be written out again:

§ 35. If a double sharp or double flat is modified to a single sharp or flat, the modification is not done according to the old practice of using two signs, a natural plus an accidental. Only the new accidental need be written out:

§ 36. Some examples of correct and incorrect placing of accidentals:

incorrect   correct
                   incorrect   correct

incorrect   correct

incorrect   correct

The last two examples show that the prolongation dots of a closely neighboring part — the lower part in the examples — are placed near the lower, not the upper, part of the note-head. In this way, there can be no question about which note is dotted.

§ 37. In sections without barlines — i.e. in cadenzas — each accidental must be written out whenever it occurs, regardless of whether it has already been noted. An exception is made for immediate repetition of the modified note:

§ 38. A trill within a measure is indicated simply with the sign: tr. A wavy line is not necessary.

§ 39. When a trill is long, sounding through several measures, tr is written above the first note, and beginning there a wavy line is drawn above all the measures of the trilled note. All notes under the wavy line are to be connected with a tie. This is important, because without this, the first beat of each bar during the trill could easily receive an unwanted accent:

When the trill is continued on a new line or a new page, the tr sign should be *not* repeated, the note need only be tied as described previously, and above it, the wavy line continued from the previous line or page, beginning *before* the note, all the way through to the end of the trill. The end of the trill is indicated by a downward stroke at the end of the wavy line:

§ 40. The identity or alteration of a trill's auxiliary note can be indicated next to or above the tr sign with a small accidental, or else with a small stemless note-head in parentheses, next to the principal note:

§ 41. In orchestral parts for high woodwinds, the octave sign should not be used too often. Despite the many leger lines, the actual position of the note is preferable. In full score, where space is not available for many leger lines, the octave sign is permissible:

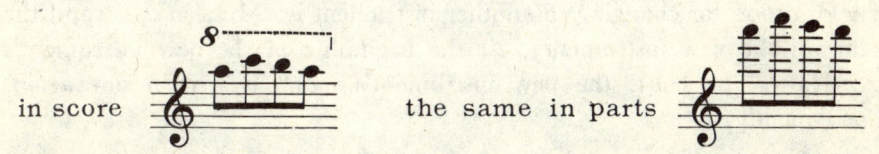

in score   the same in parts

§ 42. On a new page (or successive pages) of a full score an *a 2* ("a due") sign indicated on the previous page must be written in parentheses if the two players *continue playing* the same part in unison, until their parts become separated again:

line end

line beginning
(a2)

This indication is used at the beginning of each "broken score" (i.e. two or more braces on one page) when needed.

§ 43. Orchestral parts should always have appropriate cues written in small notes. This applies specially to material with complex rhythms, where even after a few bars the player might need orientation as to how far along the ensemble may be. The copyist should choose carefully from the score cues that would be clearly heard by the player and have conspicuous, identifiable rhythm. The instrument playing the cue must be indicated with small notes. The cue must always be written in the clef and transposition which is being read by the guided player. It is important that this guidance must not consist of only one or two notes, but enough for the player to have time to identify the part and follow it for a little while. When there is a long pause of many measures, guidance should be given again and again at various intervals of time:

§ 44. It often happens with woodwinds that the player has to change his instrument, e.g. the 2nd Flute changes to Piccolo, the English horn to 2nd Oboe, etc. Such change must be indicated in the score or part as soon as the actual playing on the first instrument stops and is followed by a pause. (N.B. There should be sufficient time to make the change of instruments.) Any change of key signature that may be required for the new instrument should also be made at this point, and if cues are needed here they should be written in according to the new key of the new instrument. The direction for changing to another instrument is: Muta in . . . (and the name of the new instrument). At the beginning of the new instrument's part (after the cue), the new instrument's name is written out again. Consequently:

incorrect

correct

§ 45. For percussion instruments without identifiable pitch, there is no clef and key signature at the beginning of the staff. These instruments are used only to emphasize the rhythm, they cannot be tuned, so they do not require clef and key signature. When the usual stick is to be changed, the indication concerning the type of stick to be used by the player should be written at the beginning of the line. The customary indications are as follows:

    a) With a soft stick = colla bacchetta di timpani

    b) With a wooden stick = colla bacchetta di tamburo

    c) With a metal stick = colla bacchetta di triangolo

    d) With a bass drum stick = colla bacchetta di gran cassa.

For each percussion instrument used, a specific space on the staff is assigned, and kept throughout the composition. For example, if the first space is chosen for the bass drum, each time the bass drum is used in the composition, it is always written in the first space. Its note stems are always drawn in the same direction. In a printed score, naturally, these notes are not written on a staff but on a single line. As a very general rule, composers only use four instruments of indefinite pitch: the triangle, the cymbals, the snare or one of the smaller drums, and the bass drum. These can be conveniently placed on two staves (from top to bottom, according to their "pitch"):

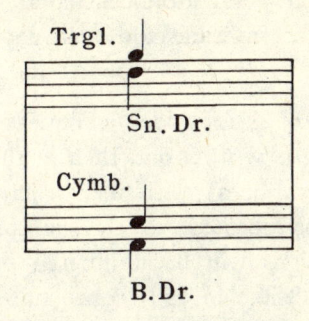

§ 46. When many percussion instruments are used (or even a few), it is best to write their parts on separate staves in the manner of a full score. In such percussion-instrument scores the kettle drums are always placed first, at the top, the others underneath in their appropriate places (see § 29). The xylophone, glockenspiel, and other instruments with identifiable pitches, are put into this score also. The individual instruments should be indicated at the point of their entries. Playing the piece, each percussionist gets such a score. Consequently, there must be as many scores available as players necessary for performance. Experience has proved that such percussion scores provide a greater measure of safety for the percussionists than individual parts do, inasmuch as each performer can take in at a glance the activity of the entire percussion group:

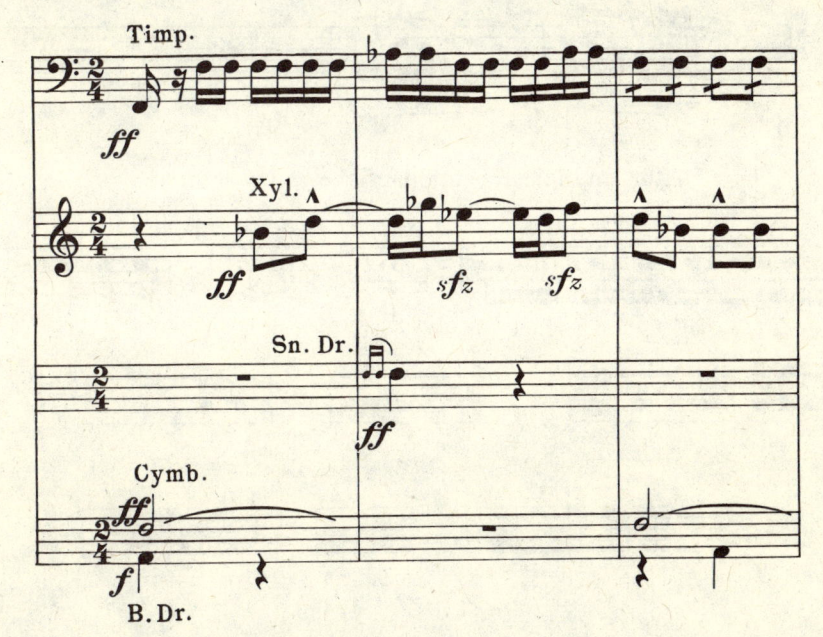

§ 47. *Individual* — that is, unconventional — abbreviations should not be used in musical notation. Casual, improvised abbreviations are difficult to figure out, they are easily misunderstood, and sources of serious mistakes. This is particularly true of full scores. Not only the conductor but the copyist may get lost in a maze of numbers, letters, colorful indications, etc. Certain abbreviations are permissible and even necessary. Among them are the following:

a) The abbreviation of simple, identical measures in individual parts. First the whole bar must be written out, then at the end of the measure (if followed by several identical ones) a number in parentheses, indicating how many times this bar will be repeated (see the example below). The following bars with abbreviation signs will be numbered on top. This method of abbreviation is also permissible in full scores, naturally without the numberings:

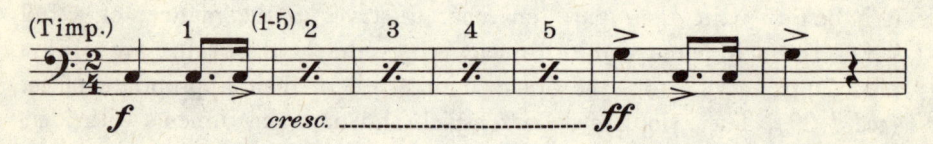

b) The repetition of two bars in individual parts at the beginning of a line, to which the performer's eye can easily refer. This abbreviation is indicated by two parallel diagonal lines across the *third* barline, with a single dot on either side. This means that the *first* two bars are to be repeated, naturally with all their performance indications:

c) The sign for multiple repetition of the same note:

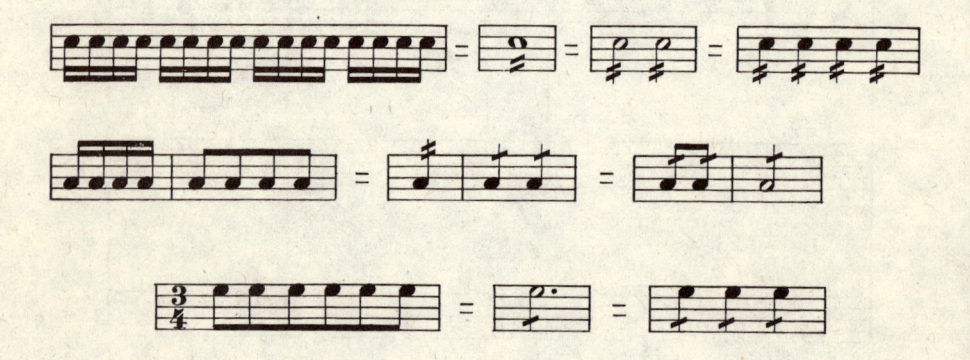

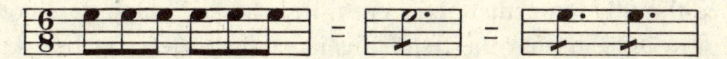

Each of these repetitions can be used with an eighth, sixteenth, thirty-second, or sixty-fourth beam, also in full score. For abbreviation of the tremolo, see below.

d) The sign for repetition *within* the measure of a single unified figure is a thick line, leaning to the right in the middle of the staff, without dots. Also usable in full score:

e) In popular-music notation, repetitions of the same chord within one bar:

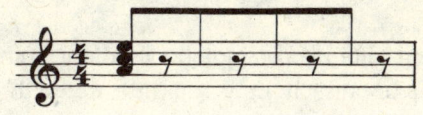

This method is also occasionally used in symphonic scores. It may be used in manuscript, but in print the complete musical notation is better. The same applies to all the other abbreviations treated in this §.

§ 48. Current notation of the tremolo differs in certain ways from the former manner. Frequently the notes of the tremolo — whether in a single voice or in a chord-tremolo — must be written far from each other, because at the same time another part might be in considerable motion, with many notes having to be written out. The old notation had only a symbol of a beam between the tremolo notes, and was consequently confusing when for example notes were placed as follows in 4/4:

When such 16th tremolos are in even rhythm (with no dotted notes among them) modern notation represents them with 8ths. In this way the units of the measure show more clearly and look more connected (two eighths = one quarter):

Above the 8th beam there is a *short* 16th beam, which does not reach the stems, to indicate that the tremolo is in 16ths. Care must be taken that the 16th beam does not touch the stems, because if it does, the tremolo will change into two simple 16ths! The notation of the previous figure's tremolo in 32nds is as follows:

If the tremolo is **faster** than this, i.e. not to be counted, but free, in addition to the 32nd beaming the word *"trem."* should be written. The indication for a 32nd tremolo for the duration of an eighth note (two 16ths = one 8th):

The older notation should also not be used for tremolos lasting longer than dotted quarters, because it may separate notes to the point of illegibility, as in the following example:

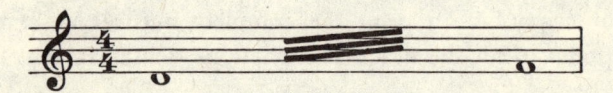

Present-day notation divides such whole notes into two half notes, indicating tremolo on the half note, and connects the notes with a slur:

Such notation can be better placed in the measure, and consequently is more readable. The tremolos of the last example can also be used with dotted values.

§ 49. Change of clef in a part must be written immediately before the note (a few exceptions to this rule will be noted below). The new clef remains valid until the next change, even though the part might be having a rest:

If the clef change is preceded by a simple barline without key signature, the new clef is written before it, regardless of whether the validity of the new clef begins on a new line or new page:

In cases of shorter than quarter rests the change of clef is not indicated before the note but before the sign of the rest, in fact before a fraction of its value. In this way the connection of the fraction-values will be more conspicuous:

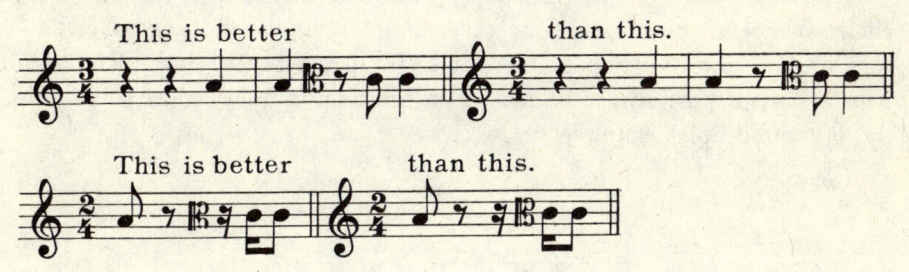

In full scores and parts, change of clef is indicated at the end of a line only when the following line bears no signature (key and time) but the clef itself.

If there are time and key signatures besides change of clef, they are to be indicated as in the examples below:

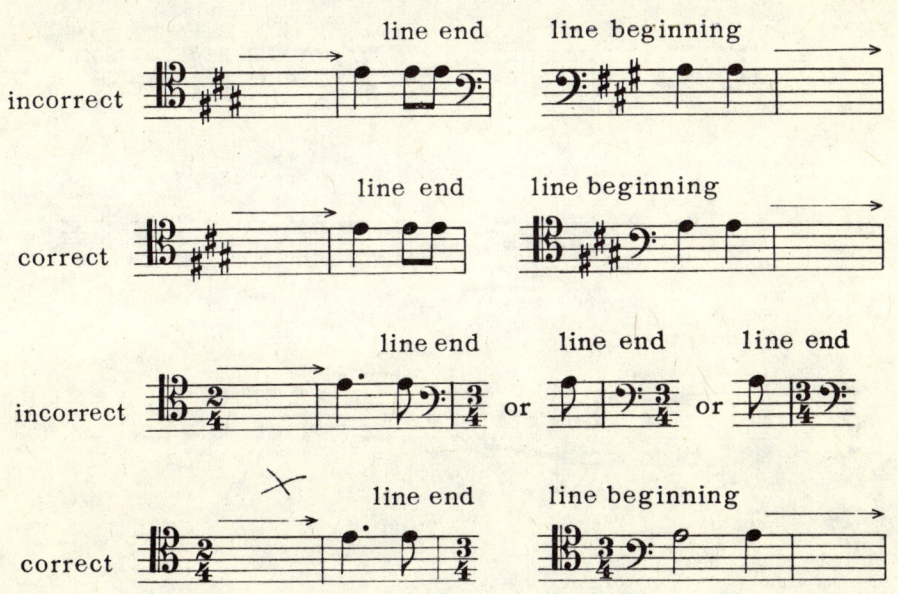

§ 50. Duplets, triplets, quadruplets, etc. are also written differently from the way they used to be. According to the old method, the number indicating the division of time value (2, 3, 4, etc.) was close to the note-head, and the notes or figure were put under a slur. This just added to the ambiguity of possible interpretation of the slur (see page 2). Often the slurs were omitted and only the number was written. This, in turn, was often confused with fingerings; differentiation between roman and italicized numbers was not enough. In modern notation, if the beaming shows the metric grouping clearly, no brackets are used and the number is placed close to the beam, at the middle of the figure, even when the beam contains various note values. If there are no beams, or if the beaming does not indicate the metric grouping clearly enough, broken brackets are used, enclosing the number. These brackets are written usually *above the staff* regardless of the direction of the stems. If such a bracket would interfere with a slur, it must always be placed on the side opposite to the slur (as in the last quadruplet example below).

When two brackets are used in a combination of the above, they should always be parallel one above the other:

§ 51. There is only one rule for the notation of grace notes: the slur, tying the small notes to the principal one, must not interfere with leger lines, as in the example below:

Generally it does not matter whether the stems and slurs of small notes are above or below, but it is more proper to put the slurs above, no matter where the stems may be. If the stems of the principal and grace notes are directed the same way, the rule in § 17 may be considered decisive. In general it is best to treat the small notes as if they had proper values. Some examples of placing grace notes (compare page 6):

The termination slur of a trill is somewhat more important, because the principal note is often placed far from its written-out termination. This termination may consist of one or more notes, but that makes no difference to the placing of the slur:

acceptable   correct   obsolete

§ 52. Indications that confuse the score-reader or copyist should be avoided, as for example in the Oboe part: "col Viol. II. Oct. Bassa"; in the Flute part: "col Viol. I. Oct. Alta," and so on. Repeat signs should be avoided when they involve only a few bars, or when within the section to be repeated changes are to be made during the repeat, as in the following example, which was taken from a printed part:

To the inexperienced performer this example can be confusing to the point of obscurity, because the signs do not make clear at a glance, as they should, that the last measure must be played piano the first time but forte in the repetition, and that in the repetition the first three measures are silent. Indications causing such reading difficulty and confusion — and even more in full scores — are annoying and time-wasting for copyists, editors, conductors, and in last analysis also for the composer himself. Experience shows that these are the source of most mistakes in performance. Manuscripts to be published should be especially clear, understandable, and free from impractical abbreviations. The clear, simple, and correct notation of the example above is as follows:

§ 53. If possible, never write a string solo on the same staff with the tutti. It is better to bring together other parts when there is insufficient space for the solo part. The 1st and 2nd violin parts could be written easily on the same staff, as could the 'cello and double bass. With these contractions we already make available two extra staves.

Consequently, if one of the string parts in a full score has a solo, a new staff should be started for it. The name of the instrument should be written above it, as well as the direction: *solo* or *sola* (if two or more soloists play:

soli or *sole*), and above the old staff: *altri* (= the others). The two or more staves are connected with the appropriate braces as follows:

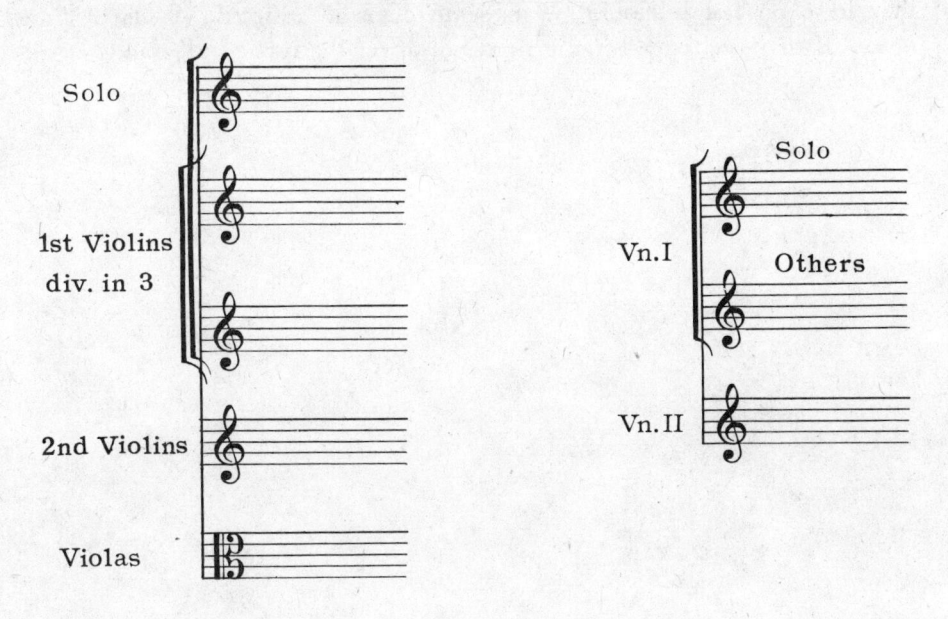

At the end of the solo, the indication "col tutti" or just "tutti" is written to indicate that the soloist or soloists are to rejoin the others. At such times, naturally, the tutti part is also written out on the solo staff, and on the following page the solo staff is discontinued.

§ 54. Before writing out the individual parts, scores should be given numbers or letters, the so-called rehearsal numbers or letters. The numbering should be done by the composer if possible. Well-placed numbers make rehearsal easier. In the parts, numbers (or letters) should be prominently placed, if possible framed in a conspicuous color. Care should be taken that the numbers come at the *beginning* of the measure and *not over the barline:*

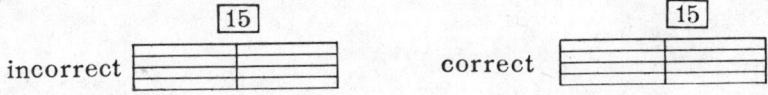

§ 55. At the end of the odd-numbered (right-hand) pages of individual parts there should always be a rest, enabling the player to turn the page without haste. This is especially important for parts used by a single player. With strings, where two players use one part, as a last resort one player can turn the page while the other continues to play. In such cases, however, care should be taken that not all of those playing one part, e.g. 1st violins, will have to turn at the same time. It is not a matter of indifference if of

14 1st violins only seven play at the same time, while the other seven are busy turning the page. In the copying of parts, the ends of the pages — if they have no rest — should be made to come at different points of the music. If they are, page-turning need not affect the orchestral sound.

TABLES

1. Terminology of

Values	English American	British
𝍝	Whole note	Semibreve
▬	Whole rest	Semibreve rest
𝅗𝅥	Half note	Minim
▬	Half rest	Minim rest
♩	Quarter note	Crotchet
𝄽	Quarter rest	Crotchet rest
♪	Eighth note	Quaver
𝄾	Eighth rest	Quaver rest
𝅘𝅥𝅯	Sixteenth note	Semiquaver
𝄿	Sixteenth rest	Semiquaver rest
𝅘𝅥𝅰	Thirty-second note	Demisemiquaver
𝅀	Thirty-second rest	Demisemiquaver rest
𝅘𝅥𝅱	Sixty-fourth note	Hemidemisemiquaver
𝅁	Sixty-fourth rest	Hemidemisemiquaver rest

Note Values and Rests

German	Italian	French	Latin
Ganze Note	Semibreve	Ronde	Semibrevis
Ganze Pause	Pausa di semibreve	Pause	Semipausa
Halbe Note	Minima	Blanche	Minima
Halbe Pause	Pausa di minima	Demi-pause	Pausa minima
Viertelnote	Semiminima	Noire	Semiminima
Viertelpause	Pausa di semiminima	Soupir	Suspirium
Achtelnote	Croma	Croche	Fusa
Achtelpause	Pausa di croma	Demi-soupir	Semisuspirium
Sechzehntelnote	Semicroma	Double croche	Semifusa
Sechzehntelpause	Pausa di semicroma	Quart de soupir	Pausa semifusa
Zweiunddreissigstelnote	Biscroma	Triple croche	Subsemifusa
Zweiunddreissigstelpause	Pausa di biscroma	Huitième de soupir	Pausa subsemifusa
Vierundsechzigstel-note	Semibiscroma	Quadruple croche	Fusella
Vierundsechzigstel-pause	Pausa di semibiscroma	Seizième de soupir	Pausa fusella

2. The Names and Symbols for Octaves

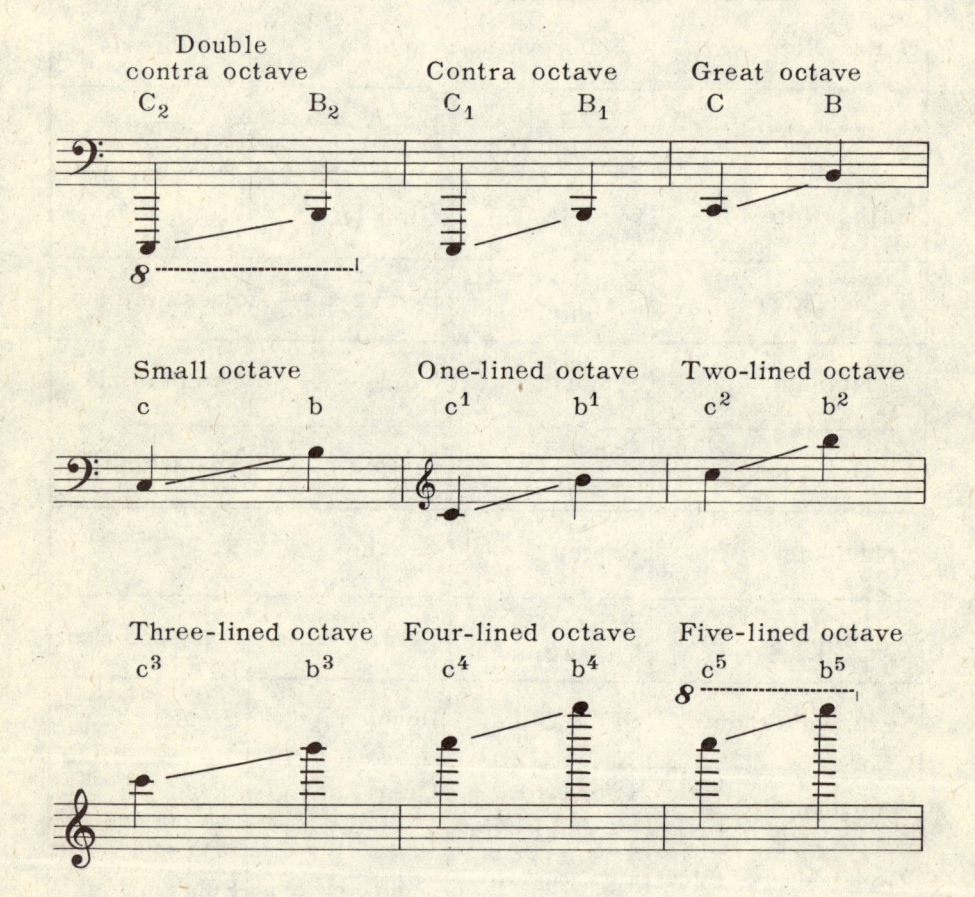

Double contra octave: C_2 B_2
Contra octave: C_1 B_1
Great octave: C B

Small octave: c b
One-lined octave: c^1 b^1
Two-lined octave: c^2 b^2

Three-lined octave: c^3 b^3
Four-lined octave: c^4 b^4
Five-lined octave: c^5 b^5

3. The Division of Note Values

			𝅗𝅥	♩	♪	𝅘𝅥𝅯	𝅘𝅥𝅰	𝅘𝅥𝅱	𝅘𝅥𝅲
𝅝	1/1	=	2/2	4/4	8/8	16/16	32/32	64/64	128/128
𝅗𝅥	1/2	=	---	2/4	4/8	8/16	16/32	32/64	64/128
♩	1/4	=	---	---	2/8	4/16	8/32	16/64	32/128
♪	1/8	=	---	---	---	2/16	4/32	8/64	16/128
𝅘𝅥𝅯	1/16	=	---	---	---	---	2/32	4/64	8/128
𝅘𝅥𝅰	1/32	=	---	---	---	---	---	2/64	4/128
𝅘𝅥𝅱	1/64	=	---	---	---	---	---	---	2/128

4. General View of the Keys and Key Signatures

Key Signature	English	Italian	French	German
	C major A minor	Do maggiore La minore	Ut majeur La mineur	C Dur A Moll
	G major E minor	Sol maggiore Mi minore	Sol majeur Mi mineur	G Dur E Moll
	D major B minor	Re maggiore Si minore	Re majeur Si mineur	D Dur H Moll
	A major F-sharp minor	La maggiore Fa diesis minore	La majeur Fa dièse mineur	A Dur Fis Moll
	E major C-sharp minor	Mi maggiore Do diesis minore	Mi majeur Ut dièse mineur	E Dur Cis Moll
	B major G-sharp minor	Si maggiore Sol diesis minore	Si majeur Sol dièse mineur	H Dur Gis Moll
	F-sharp major D-sharp minor	Fa diesis maggiore Re diesis minore	Fa dièse majeur Ré dièse mineur	Fis Dur Dis Moll

	English	Italian	French	German
	C-sharp major A-sharp minor	Do diesis maggiore La diesis minore	Ut dièse majeur La dièse mineur	Cis Dur Ais Moll
	F major D minor	Fa maggiore Re minore	Fa majeur Ré mineur	F Dur D Moll
	B-flat major G minor	Si bemolle maggiore Sol minore	Si bémol majeur Sol mineur	B Dur G Moll
	E-flat major C minor	Mi bemolle maggiore Do minore	Mi bémol majeur Ut mineur	Es Dur C Moll
	A-flat major F minor	La bemolle maggiore Fa minore	La bémol majeur Fa mineur	As Dur F Moll
	D-flat major B-flat minor	Re bemolle maggiore Si bemolle minore	Ré bémol majeur Si bémol mineur	Des Dur B Moll
	G-flat major E-flat minor	Sol bemolle maggiore Mi bemolle minore	Sol bémol majeur Mi bémol mineur	Ges Dur Es Moll
	C-flat major A-flat minor	Do bemolle maggiore La bemolle minore	Ut bémol majeur La bémol mineur	Ces Dur As Moll

5. The Location of Key Signatures on the Staff in Alto, Tenor, and Bass Clefs

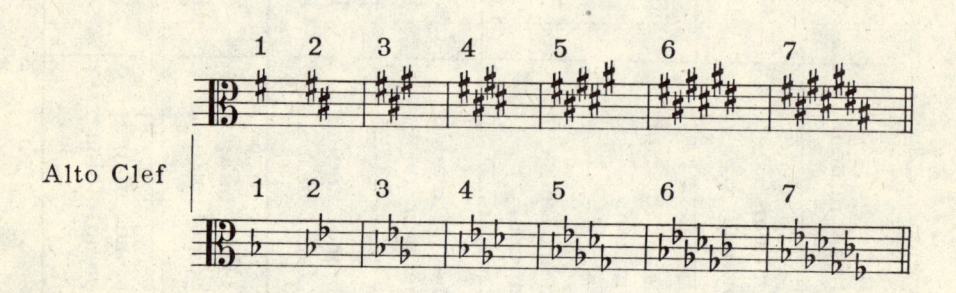

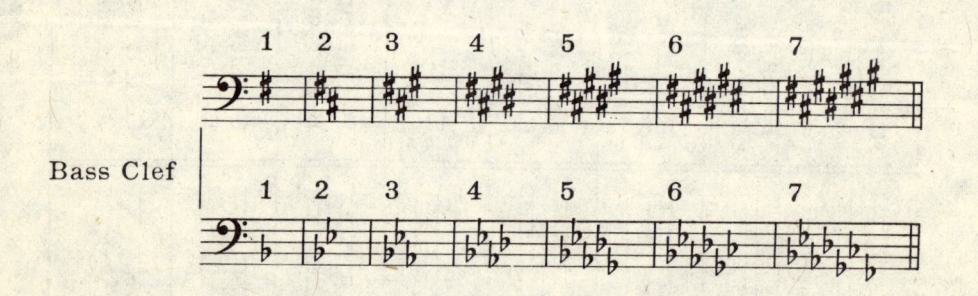

Alto Clef

Tenor Clef

Bass Clef

6. Transposing Table of Modal Scales

Key signature	Dorian	Phrygian	Lydian	Mixolydian	Aeolian	Ionian
6♯	G-sharp	A-sharp	B	C-sharp	D-sharp	F-sharp
5♯	C-sharp	D-sharp	E	F-sharp	G-sharp	B
4♯	F-sharp	G-sharp	A	B	C-sharp	E
3♯	B	C-sharp	D	E	F-sharp	A
2♯	E	F-sharp	G	A	B	D
1♯	A	B	C	D	E	G
Final	D	E	F	G	A	C
1♭	G	A	B-flat	C	D	F
2♭	C	D	E-flat	F	G	B-flat
3♭	F	G	A-flat	B-flat	C	E-flat
4♭	B-flat	C	D-flat	E-flat	F	A-flat
5♭	E-flat	F	G-flat	A-flat	B-flat	D-flat
6♭	A-flat	B-flat	C-flat	D-flat	E-flat	G-flat

Index of Signs

Sign	Page	Sign	Page	Sign	Page
·	1, 8	ṗ ↱	16	⊓	8
'	1, 8	✗	16	V	8
–	2, 8	◿	16	⊣	8
-̇ ·	9	≀	10, 16, 19	♭	8
·.·.·	9	↑≀	10, 19	→	8
‿ ‐ ‐	9	↓≀	19	←	8
>	2	↑≀	19	↑↓↑↓	10
∧ V	2	↓≀	19	♩ ♩	20
⌒ ⌒	2	tr	6, 16	+	14, 16
<>	3	♩ ♪	6	∧	22
◇♩	14	♩ ♪	6	U	22
‖: :‖	4	♩ ♫ ♩	6	U∧ ∧U	22
‖: :‖: :‖	4	♩ ♫ ♩	6	∧ U ∧ / ∧ ∧ U	22
℅	4	gliss.		fp	2
✤	4	♩ ↱	10	sfz	2
1. 2.	5	♩ ♩	21	fz	2
8------⌐	5	♩♩♩♩	21	rfz	2
8------⌐	5	[	11, 20	D.C.	4
15------⌐	5	⌐⌐	21	⊕ ※	4
15------⌐	5	℘. - ℘ed.	21	D.S.	4
◠◠ ♩♩	14	✳	21	pizz.	10, 11
◠◠ ♩♩ 3 3	14	⋀ ⋀	21	arco	10, 11
♩̌	16	𝄞	7	pizz.⦃	10
♩̰	16	Flutter	14
♫♩ ♫♩	16	con sord. (Winds)	15
♩	16	senza sord. (Winds)	15
		○	8, 14, 21	sord. (Percussion)	16
				I·II·III·IV	12, 27

General Index

"a due" (a 2) 47
Abbreviations 50
Accidentals 44
Alto clef 66
Appoggiatura 6, 55
Arco 10
Arpeggio 9, 17, 19

Bass clarinet 25
Bass clef 66
Bass drum 17, 30
Bassoon 26
Beams 33, 34

Celesta 17, 30
Change of clef 52
Change of key signature 43
Change of instrument 48
Clarinets 24
Col legno 12
Con sordino 13 (strings), 15 (brass), 16 (timpani)
Coperto 16
Crescendo 3
Cues 47
Cymbals 18, 30

Da capo 4
Dal segno 4
Damper pedal 22
Decrescendo 3
Détaché 8
Dot 1, 35, 46
Double bass 8, 28
Double bassoon 26
Double repetition mark 4
Double tonguing 14
Down bow 8
Duplets 54
Dynamic indications 36, 41, 42, 43

English horn 24
Expression marks 35, 36

Flags 34
Flute 23
Flutter-tonguing 15
Frog 8

Glissando 16, 17, 20
Glockenspiel 16, 29
Gong 18, 30
Grace notes 55

Half-spiccato 9
Half-tenuto 9

Harmonics 8
Harp 20, 21, 28
Harpsichord 28
Heel (organ notation) 22
High school voice parts 31, 32
Horn 15, 26

Kettle drum—See Timpani

Left-hand pizzicato 11
Legato 2, 37, 39
Let vibrate 20
Louré 9
Lower half of the bow 8

Marcato 2
Martellato 8
Messa di voce 15
Mixed choruses 31
Muta in 48
Muted tones (horn) 15

"Neutral" line 33
Non arpeggio 20
Numbering of strings 12, 27

Oboe 23
Octave sign 5, 47
Open (horn, trumpet) 15
Open string 8
Organ 22, 28

Page turn 57
Pedaling 21 (piano), 22 (organ)
Percussion parts 48
Piccolo 23
Pizzicato 10, 11
Pointe d'archet 36
Prima volta — Seconda volta 5

Quadruplets 54
Quintuplets 55

Rehearsal numbers 57
Repeat of bar(s) 4, 50
Repetition marks 4, 44, 50, 51
Rests 33, 41
Ricochet 9
Rinforzando 2
Rolls 16, 17, 18
Rubbed together (cymbals) 18

Saltato 9
Saxophones 25

Secco 8, 16, 17, 18
Senza sordino 13 (strings), 15 (winds)
Sextuplets 55
Sforzato 2
Shaking (tambourine) 18
Single tonguing 14
Slur 2, 37, 38, 39, 40, 41
Snare drum 17, 30
Solo (string part) 56
Spacing 42
Spiccato 8
Staccato 1, 9
Staccatissimo 1
Stems 33, 34, 35
Stopped tones 15
Struck together (cymbals) 18
Suffocato 16, 17, 18
Sul ponticello 12
Sul tasto 12
"Suspended" note 34, 37

Tambourine 18, 30
Tenor drum 17, 30
Tenor clef 7, 66
Tenuto 2
Terminology 23-31, 60, 64
Tie 2, 37, 38
Timpani 16, 29
Tip of the bow 8
Toe (organ notation) 22
Tre corde 22
Tremolo 11, 16, 17, 18, 36, 51
Triangle 17, 30
Trill 6, 17, 46, 55
Triple tonguing 14
Triplets 54
Trombone 15, 27
Trumpet 15, 26
Tuba 15, 27
Two parts on same line 33, 38, 41
Two sticks 16
Tutti 57

Una corda 22
Up bow 8
Upper half of the bow 8

Vibraphone 17, 29
Viola 8, 27
Violin 8, 27
Violoncello 8, 27
Vocal parts 3, 34, 35, 41

Xylophone 17, 29